The
NEW
RULES
for
Mortgages

Dale Robyn Siegel

ALPHA

A member of Penguin Group (USA) Inc.

ALPHA BOOKS

Published by the Penguin Group

Penguin Group (USA) Inc., 375 Hudson Street, New York, New York 10014, USA

Penguin Group (Canada), 90 Eglinton Avenue East, Suite 700, Toronto, Ontario M4P 2Y3, Canada (a division of Pearson Penguin Canada Inc.)

Penguin Books Ltd., 80 Strand, London WC2R 0RL, England

Penguin Ireland, 25 St. Stephen's Green, Dublin 2, Ireland (a division of Penguin Books Ltd.)

Penguin Group (Australia), 250 Camberwell Road, Camberwell, Victoria 3124, Australia (a division of Pearson Australia Group Pty. Ltd.)

Penguin Books India Pvt. Ltd., 11 Community Centre, Panchsheel Park, New Delhi—110 017, India

Penguin Group (NZ), 67 Apollo Drive, Rosedale, North Shore, Auckland 1311, New Zealand (a division of Pearson New Zealand Ltd.)

Penguin Books (South Africa) (Pty.) Ltd., 24 Sturdee Avenue, Rosebank, Johannesburg 2196, South Africa

Penguin Books Ltd., Registered Offices: 80 Strand, London WC2R 0RL, England

International Standard Book Number: 978-1-59257-948-8
Library of Congress Catalog Card Number: 2009923298

11   10   09   8   7   6   5   4   3   2   1

Interpretation of the printing code: The rightmost number of the first series of numbers is the year of the book's printing; the rightmost number of the second series of numbers is the number of the book's printing. For example, a printing code of 09-1 shows that the first printing occurred in 2009.

Printed in the United States of America

Note: This publication contains the opinions and ideas of its author. It is intended to provide helpful and informative material on the subject matter covered. It is sold with the understanding that the author and publisher are not engaged in rendering professional services in the book. If the reader requires personal assistance or advice, a competent professional should be consulted.

The author and publisher specifically disclaim any responsibility for any liability, loss, or risk, personal or otherwise, which is incurred as a consequence, directly or indirectly, of the use and application of any of the contents of this book.

Trademarks: All terms mentioned in this book that are known to be or are suspected of being trademarks or service marks have been appropriately capitalized. Alpha Books and Penguin Group (USA) Inc. cannot attest to the accuracy of this information. Use of a term in this book should not be regarded as affecting the validity of any trademark or service mark.

Most Alpha books are available at special quantity discounts for bulk purchases for sales promotions, premiums, fund-raising, or educational use. Special books, or book excerpts, can also be created to fit specific needs.

For details, write: Special Markets, Alpha Books, 375 Hudson Street, New York, NY 10014.

Dedicated to:
L. Herbert Siegel
My father, my mentor, my friend

Contents

Introduction

A mortgage is a tool we use to borrow money while using real property as security for the debt. The term "mortgage" is used when purchasing a new home or using real estate you already own for the equity. There are several parts to a mortgage and many documents that need to be signed, but the whole is referred to as a mortgage.

The word "mortgage" comes from both the Old French ("mort") and English ("gage") meaning "dead pledge." In the late twelfth century, the first mortgages were recorded in England. One would borrow money to buy property if they could not afford to pay all cash. If they did not pay up, the creditor would take the real estate, and therefore the property ownership would be *dead* to them. On the flip side, if a debtor paid off the loan, the debt would be extinguished and therefore *dead* in that respect.

This system was brought to America with the pilgrims, and as people bought property they would take out a loan from a bank. In those days, the banks were smart and the buyer had to put down 40 to 50 percent of the purchase price and pay back the loan over a shorter period, less than 10 years. Property ownership was nationwide by the early 1900s when the Depression hit. The government, the people, and the banks all went belly up and it was foreclosure city!

When Roosevelt became president, he created the FHA (Federal Housing Administration) to insure banks in case of default. This made lenders more apt to lend to people and not worry about foreclosure. However, the lending system was more local and each area had its own economy and based rates and lending on that.

Come on down, Fannie Mae! In 1938, the federal government created Federal National Mortgage Association (FNMA), also known as Fannie Mae, to buy mortgages from the lenders. Fannie Mae would buy the loans and sell them as securities on Wall Street. This way, the lenders had a central location to sell their loans to with a conforming set of guidelines to meet. After World War II, the veterans returned looking for housing and work and so the boom started. In 1944, The Veteran's Administration was started to insure loans taken out by veterans and their families. Not only did the government (partially) guarantee these loans, but they were 100 percent financing. Come 1970, the government realized they needed more funding for loans and created the Federal Home Loan Mortgage Corporation (FHLMC), known as Freddie Mac. Freddie would buy the loans that Fannie Mae would buy and then some. Freddie was known for doing all sorts of weird and commercial loans in addition to the basics. For instance, Freddie would buy multi-million-dollar loans used to finance co-op conversions in Manhattan, big commercial retail projects, and health facilities … more of a real estate boom.

So you can see how housing was able to progress from the caves and huts of simpler times. There will always be housing booms and bubbles that move with the nation's economy. The difference we are seeing now is that there is a global ripple effect from the bulk sale of mortgages. Since Fannie Mae, the mortgage industry became an investment vehicle for Wall Street and now the global financial world. Here we are again.

FYI: I am a huge history buff. If I were writing a different book, I would have gleefully started with the caveman.

Why I Wrote This Book

Did you notice …

- Most how-to books lately are written by hired writers and not active professionals or educators.

- Most how-to books are too long, too wordy, and just plain too much (I have been told I am long-winded).

- Most how-to books give you every little detail, as if you were performing the surgery yourself.

- Real estate how-to books are often written as state-specific guidelines and, as such, much of the content doesn't pertain to most of the readers.

Do you want …

- A how-to book on mortgages written by someone who not only helps people obtain mortgages for a living but knows how to teach it?

- To read a how-to book that has just the facts and the vocabulary you need to understand the subject matter?

- To read a how-to book that gives you short explanations for the basics and empowers you on the topic?

- A how-to book with access to the most current information out there?

- Your how-to book on mortgages to educate you on the process no matter what state you live in?

If yes, then this book is for you.

So often, clients and students have told me that I should write a book ….

My name is Dale Siegel, and I am an attorney and licensed mortgage broker. I have been in the real estate industry for over 20 years and have owned a mortgage brokerage company in New York since 1996. I run a successful boutique business, and because of that, I have considerable insider knowledge.

The mortgage industry is one where a lot of money is tossed around and where sometimes hefty commissions are made. The price of your home is one thing, but how much you pay for it in the long run is quite another thing. Your home could cost you thousands more than the original price, based solely on the type of mortgage and the interest rate you secure. Avoiding this takes shopping and insider knowledge, and at times some negotiation.

Knowledge is power. Education is your tool. In this book, I will give you a down-and-dirty lesson on what you need to know before securing a mortgage or refinancing your loan.

This is nothing new to me. I give seminars on how to get a mortgage and on real estate for beginners about 100 times a year in various venues to help consumers attain healthy financial well-being. In fact, I spent the summer of 2007 traveling around the country meeting with each WNBA team to teach the players about buying real estate. Young professionals are a great audience because they believe in their futures and want to learn how to maintain control of their own destinies.

In recent years, things were going swimmingly for buyers and sellers, or so it seemed to them. Then, in August 2008, the mortgage industry collapsed almost overnight and without warning. This was shocking for so many people, but for me it was about time. Since then, so much in the industry has changed that you could write a book about it. And I have!

Using current guidelines from lenders, Fannie Mae, Freddie Mac, FHA, title companies, credit reporting agencies, appraisal companies, and legal text, I've put together this book on what *you* need to know about borrowing mortgage money. Through thousands of mortgages I have gotten for people I have learned the nuances and twists of the business. I am still learning every day and I pass on as much of the basics, new stuff, and secrets as I can cram into my allotted page limit. I do swear it is not boring!

This book is generous with information but cheap with words—or so I think. I go through the primary stuff first on credit, income, and assets. Then we swing into the process and different kinds of loans out there. All through the book, I try to spice it with a little humor and spatter stories to help you relate to the material.

Since the big mortgage industry implosion, the rules have changed for so many things, from credit reports to loan amounts. I rewrote and edited the material many times, as these changes came about since the end of 2008. The rules of borrowing mortgage money have stabilized into the new industry standard. What we are seeing now are simply procedural changes that affect how the banks process the loans but not how they approve borrowers. I can assure the reader that much of the material will remain current. However, I vowed to keep my readers, students, and clients up-to-date on the nuances. Therefore, please check my blog, www.dalesiegel.com, regularly to see what is going on in *The New Rules for Mortgages*. I am honored to have written this book and proud of the content and information disbursed. More so, I am proud of you, the reader, for taking the initiative to read it and empower yourselves with the knowledge.

Acknowledgments

I would like to thank several people both integral in getting this book to print and for their support. First, I must thank my friend Ellice Uffer from IBM Press for encouraging me to write the final draft and proper book proposal and for getting it into the hands of Tom Stevens at Alpha Books. Tom Stevens, my acquisitions editor and liaison at Alpha Books, was always available to answer my questions and put me in the right direction. Megan Douglass, Kayla Dugger, and Jan Zoya deserve special thanks for editing my draft with perfection and kindness. I must thank my friend Giffy Giffoniello, who volunteered to give my book a once over before I sent it to the publisher and wound up editing it three additional times before it actually went.

I'd also like to thank David Meerman Scott and Peter Shankman, marketing geniuses, who gave me tons of ideas for creating my "platform" and getting me exposure even before I wrote the book. My assistant Anne Hiltunen and my tech guy, Tom Alongi, were both encouraging and golden in my plight to authordom, and I could not have done it without them both. A warm and loving thank you to my family and close friends for being so supportive and proud of this endeavor.

Special Thanks to the Technical Reviewer

The New Rules for Mortgages was reviewed by an expert who double-checked the accuracy of what you'll learn here, to help us ensure that this book gives you everything you need to know about mortgages. Special thanks are extended to Ginny Anderson.

Trademarks

Chapter 1

The All-Important Credit Score

During my real estate and finance seminars, I spend a lot of time on credit as part of the mortgage qualification. This is the part where the people who were sleeping perk up and become involved in the conversation. More people than not have bad credit, whether from true financial hardship or sheer sloppiness. When the economy is in trouble, it is usually because consumer spending and savings are down. Consumers stop both saving and spending when the prices of consumer goods and the cost of living go out of whack, when they lose jobs, or when they are just plain scared to part with money. Bad credit is becoming an epidemic in the United States and has far-reaching effects on many long-term needs such as homeownership, renting, borrowing, opening checking accounts, getting a job, and even insurance.

Mortgage lenders do not necessarily look at the content of your credit report, but focus on the FICO score when approving and pricing your mortgage. For the purpose of this chapter, I want you to think of the person reading and analyzing your credit report as a computer. It reads and registers but does not think. (Think of Rosie the maid in the TV show *The Jetsons*. Am I dating myself?) Thus, many of the things we talk about would not make sense if a "real" person were involved and thinking. Sorry, but this is the way it is.

Why Is the FICO Score So Important?

FICO stands for Fair Isaac & Company, the creator of the FICO scoring system. Your FICO score is a gauge used by credit companies to determine your potential risk to them if they lend money to you. This gauge rates your ability to pay your bills and your history of doing so.

There are three main credit reporting agencies in the United States: Equifax, Experian (the old TRW), and TransUnion. Each agency uses a different formula for calculating your score, so it will differ slightly for each. Scores also differ because not all the creditors report your payment history with them to each agency, and they may report at different times of the month. So not only does your score vary by agency, it varies by date. I have seen a range from 10 to 100 points either way. Therefore, lenders use the middle score to determine your interest rate—not the average, but the numerical middle.

FICO Score Example

You make a payment 30 days late to Sears. Sears reports only to Equifax, and your Equifax score is reduced from 750 to 619. Your TransUnion score is 702 and your Experian score is 776, so your middle score is 702, but it could have been higher if you had not blown off Sears.

Before you even begin searching for a home, you need to find out your credit score. This all-important number determines if you can even get a mortgage. The level of risk you pose as a borrower affects your loan amount, how much equity they will allow you to mortgage, and your interest rate. The better (higher) your FICO score, the better your overall risk assessment, and the better (lower) your rate will be.

The Better Your Credit Score, the Lower Your Interest Rate

There was never a tiered pricing range with mortgages before the big bang in the mortgage industry. If your mortgage was approved, you got the same rate as everybody else. Under the new rules for mortgages, the better your credit the lower your interest rate. Your interest rate is calculated based on your FICO score and your loan-to-value (LTV) of the mortgage. It is subjected to price tiering, which should be the same with most lenders, but ask to be safe. No matter how much equity you have in your home, a low credit score will affect your interest rate!

What Is Loan-to-Value?

The loan-to-value (LTV) is the maximum loan allowed based on a percentage of the appraised value of the home. If the maximum LTV allowed for your loan program is 90 percent, then a $100,000 home will afford a $90,000 loan.

FICO Score Loan-to-Value Adjustments*

LTV Ratios

Credit Score	<=60.00	60.01–70	70.01–75	75.01–80	80.01–85	85.01–90	90.01–95	95.01–97	97.01–100
>=740	-0.250	0.000	0.000	0.000	0.000	0.000	0.000	-0.250	NA
720–739	-0.250	0.000	0.000	0.250	0.000	0.000	0.000	-0.250	NA
700–719	-0.250	0.500	0.500	0.750	0.500	0.500	0.500	0.250	NA
680–699	0.000	0.500	1.000	1.500	1.000	0.750	0.750	0.250	NA
660–679	0.000	1.000	2.000	2.500	2.250	1.750	1.750	1.000	NA
640–659	0.500	1.250	2.500	3.000	2.750	2.250	2.250	1.500	NA
620–639	0.500	1.500	3.000	3.000	3.000	2.750	2.750	2.250	NA
<620	NA	NA	NA	NA	NA	NA	NA	NA	NA

*This chart is for purchase loans and refinances without cash back to you. These figures are subject to change. Use this as a guide but check with your lender for current adjustments.

The FICO Score Range

FICO scores range from 300 to 850, with 850 being the best. I have *heard* that the average FICO score in America is currently in the 670 range, the 720 range, and the 770 range depending on the source. I am not sure what the average is, but I bet it is much lower! I used to say that anybody could get a loan if his score was over 500, but times have changed. I also used to discuss compensating factors, which no longer mean as much, but I will still touch on them later. Now, under the new guidelines, FICO score will affect everything from type of mortgage, to your LTV, to your interest rate.

Co-Borrowers

If there are two co-borrowers, one with terrible credit and one with good credit, the person with a high FICO score will not be able to compensate for the person with the lower score. Banks base their decision on the lower score. In this case, it is best to take the person with the lower score off the deal.

What Makes Up My FICO Score?

Five factors make up your credit score:

1. *Payment history* takes into account whether or not you've paid all your bills on time and for how long. It accounts for 35 percent of your score. If you have paid one or more bills 30 days, 60 days, or 90 days late, your credit score will drop. The longer your credit history and your history of on-time payments, the better your score will be. Remember, the computer is reading this, and it likes to see at least 24 months of credit history and at least four tradelines— mortgage, car loans, and major credit cards respectively count most. Store and gas cards don't have as much pull.

Close Store Cards

Might I suggest closing all those miscellaneous store cards? You probably only got them to get the store discount on the initial purchase. You should not rack up a bunch of cards all over the place, and besides, everybody takes Visa and Mastercard now. They can adversely affect your score by being too new and having too much credit available. (The more credit you have available, the more debt you can incur.)

2. *Amounts owed* accounts for 30 percent of your score. Debt-to-credit ratio is determined by adding up all of your current outstanding balances and dividing that by available credit. Note that the computer does not like you being maxed out; it wants you owing less than 50 percent of your available credit—on each card.

    My best advice would be to have a few major credit cards and keep all of them under that 50 percent mark. I never suggest paying off your debt before you apply for a loan, because it will not make a difference. I do say make sure you know what you have, what you owe, and keep it under the 50 percent limit. I swear this can make a huge difference!

3. *Length of credit history*, the amount of time you have held each of your credit cards, counts for 15 percent of your score. Lenders want to know you can pay off debt over time. Again, the computer likes to read at least 24 months of credit history. You will not even get a score unless you have at least 6 months of active credit. However, it is better to have a few credit vehicles for 12 months than many credit vehicles for 6 months. Length of credit is more important than quantity of credit vehicles. That is why it is so important to establish credit and a good payment history early in life.

4. *New credit* counts for 10 percent of your score. Any attempts to acquire new credit (such as recent credit or loan applications) will adversely affect your score. Opening up new accounts means "I need more credit; I spend, spend, spend" to the lender, and that makes the lender nervous. If you have applied for credit and decided not to take the card, the computer will read it as if you were rejected by the creditor! Remember, you're not exactly asking the mortgage lender to fork over chump change.

5. *Type of credit* you use (credit cards, installment loans, etc.) also is a factor in determining your FICO score, although it is unclear which types hold what weight. This category counts for 10 percent of your score. A good mix is important to establish credit, but once you have a history it will be fine to close some the less-important cards (sorry Mr. Bloomingdale's). However, closed accounts may still play into your credit score.

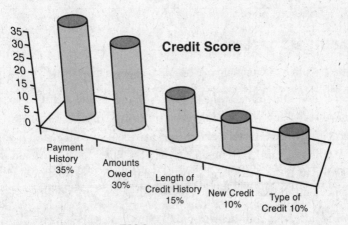

What makes up your FICO score.

Unsuited for Loan

I had a client who was borderline in obtaining a particular mortgage program with a 680 FICO score. Then, there were problems with the house she was purchasing, which took a long time to resolve, so the closing was delayed for so long that the lender had to run a new credit check. In the meantime, my client treated herself to a new Armani suit at Barney's. The salesperson enticed her with a new Barney's credit card, offering 10 percent off the suit. Of course, she took her up on it. It would save her $200. Nevertheless, in the end it cost her 12 points of her FICO. Her score dropped below what was required for this loan, and the bank rejected her. If she had put the suit on her American Express card, it would not have affected her FICO score. Why? Because she had the Amex card for years, but the Barney's card was brand-new credit and more opportunity to spend from the lender's view. Just say no to new credit!

Credit Boosters

Here are some obvious and not-so-obvious ways to improve your score:

Pay on time: Duh. One of the best ways to increase your FICO score is to start making your payments on time on a consistent basis. Remember, payment history makes up 35 percent of your score. If you have fallen behind on payments in the past, put it in the past and start fresh today. If you have large credit card debt, just pay the minimum balance on time each month, and this will boost your credit score.

Control your debt: Your debt-to-credit ratio makes up 30 percent of your FICO score. If you have a lot of debt, start paying it down and don't add to it. Keep the plastic home for a while until you get back on track. If you're having trouble paying down a credit card, think about transferring the balance to a 0 percent interest card. That way your payments will be applied to the principle balance rather than the interest. This will help you pay the credit card off faster. Before taking out a new credit card to make a transfer, call your credit company first and see if they will lower your interest rate.

Do not cancel your cards: I had a lot to say on this in the previous section. Remember, credit length makes up 15 percent of your FICO score. The older, the better.

Do not apply for more credit: If you want to improve your FICO score, do not apply for new credit cards and never apply for retail store cards. Each new application is a new inquiry that might not result in a tradeline. Each new tradeline is too new to show a history, so it is a negative rating. New credit applications make up 10 percent of your score and that is a negative effect.

Create a mix: Your credit mix makes up 10 percent of your score, so it is not a big deal. The computer likes to see that you can handle different types of credit. However, if you do not need a car, do not go out and lease one!

Credit Killers

As you can probably guess, the credit killers I'm going to discuss here fall into the five major categories that make up your FICO score.

High balances: If you have high balances on your credit cards and loans, your debt-to-credit ratio is going to be a lot higher than it should be, which will hurt your score dramatically. Try to keep all balances below 45 percent of available credit.

Late payments: If you don't make your payments on time, your credit score is going to take a major hit. You don't have to pay the whole balance at once, just the minimum balance each month. Fair Isaac has three categories for late payments: 30 days late, 60 days late, and 90 days late. Being 30 days late will drastically reduce your score, which, as you can guess, means that if you're 90 days late, your score will nosedive.

Not enough credit: The biggest credit myth is thinking you can have one credit card and make the payments in full, on time every month, and this will give you a top credit score. This is wrong. If you have only one card, your credit report will look unimpressive, as if you can't handle having credit. Creditors want to see many accounts open, being used, and being paid on time.

Length of credit history: Even if you have many accounts open, active, and being paid on time, if your credit history doesn't go back at least 12 to 24 months, your credit score won't be as high as you may anticipate. You shouldn't wait to open credit accounts until you need them; open some now and start creating a good credit score.

Closing accounts: As I said earlier, don't close your credit card accounts. The longer each account is open, the better your score. Moreover, by leaving your account open, you will be helping your debt-to-credit ratio. When people close accounts, their debt-to-credit ratios take an immediate hit, and this ratio makes up 30 percent of your score.

Errors: Mistakes happen frequently on credit reports. People have similar names, etc. Request a credit report every year and check to make sure there are no discrepancies. The biggest mistake people make is not checking their reports and finding there are blatant errors only when they go to apply for a mortgage. Unfortunately, these mistakes can take time to clear up and may interfere with your getting a mortgage or getting a lower interest rate.

Correct Credit Report Errors

You can take steps to correct errors on your credit report:

1. Contact each bureau concerning errors on accounts that have been paid or closed. Send a cover letter and any supporting documents as proof. Ask to have your report updated within the required 30-day period and ask for a revised report for your records. If they require additional information from the creditor, you will have to go after them for it.

2. While you are doing that, ask all three bureaus to remove any inquiries from your report that are more than two years old.

Too much available credit is worse than not enough credit.

Tina, attending a seminar, proudly told the class that her credit is excellent, and she is pre-approved for credit cards all the time. In fact, she has 10 credit cards with available balances of $10,000 each in her sock drawer! Of course, she says, she has never uses them but has them if need be.

Here is the problem with that: the computer and lender also see that she can use them if need be. Think about the potential borrowing power of Tina, as the bank would. Tina finds a house, qualifies, and borrows $300,000 to buy it. After she moves in she decides to re-furnish the family room, then the bedroom, and then those kitchen cabinets that look dreary. Well, let's just go to that sock drawer!

The fact is, Tina can buy a house, take out a $300,000 mortgage, and then potentially bang up $100,000 in credit card debt. This will push her over the qualifying edge, and she might stop making all payments. What if she lost her job or went through all of her savings and then there was nothing left? Having too much credit available is a time bomb waiting to happen. Do not apply for and get too many credit cards. Close out extra credit cards that you will never use, and certainly close out the newer cards without any proven history.

Because we now know what makes up your score and the weight each item is given, prioritize your actions:

- Pay your bills on time.
- Keep the amount owed under 50 percent of high limit.
- Keep your oldest accounts in the best shape.
- Don't apply for more credit.
- Keep a healthy mix of credit only if you need it.

Closing Out Unwanted Credit Cards

The worst thing you can do is close the wrong credit account. A bad account to close is one that you have had for a long time or one that you still owe money to. The credit cards with the longest history have the greatest positive effect for you. Again, if you have a credit card and do not want it anymore, simply pay it off and leave it dormant. If you close a card with a balance due, it appears as if the creditor cut you off, not that it was your choice. The computer reads it as *closed by credit grantor*, which will negatively impact your score. Thus, zero out the card first and then decide if you should close it.

If you want to close a credit card because you think you have too many open and fear the lender may think you have access to too much credit, choose carefully. Close the newer cards first, as they have the least history. Then close out the retail and gas cards because they have the lowest priority. Keep the major credit cards, pay down balances, and don't use them for a while.

If you want to close the card because you finally paid it off and don't want to be tempted to go into debt again, just cut the card up or hide it in your sock drawer. That way you won't be tempted to use it anymore, yet the card is still activated and will help boost your debt-to-credit ratio and credit length. Remember, the longer you hold accounts in good standing, the better your score will be. While closing cards, refrain from opening new ones, because this will counteract what you are trying to achieve.

Inquiries

An inquiry on your credit report appears when a potential creditor runs a credit check to see if you qualify for a loan or credit card. To the computer, it looks like you are in need of money. The computer will try to match up the inquiry with a new active tradeline. If it cannot, then it assumes the creditor rejected you, not that you decided not to go through with it. I told you, it does not think!

Unfortunately, inquiries stay on your credit report for 24 months, and it is your responsibility to ask the credit agencies to remove the inquiry after that period of time.

So, when reviewing your credit report, check out the inquiry section and draw a line after 24 months. Make a list of the old ones and send it to the bureaus to remove. Always ask for a copy of the updated credit report.

There are two major fallacies about inquires. One is that multiple inquires that run in the same industry count as one. The other is that all inquires in a 30-day period count as one. These cannot possibly be true. Each lender uses a different credit service company to obtain its credit reports. Each inquiry shows up as a different name such as CBC, INFO1, CIS, TRANSUNION, etc. The inquiry only reports the company it came from, not the reason. How can the computer distinguish between a car and a mortgage? The computer cannot read each inquiry as a request for the same type of credit. Nor will it bundle all your inquiries in one month into one.

My students always complain that companies are looking into their credit without permission. When they get crazy, I say chill out and read below.

Potential creditor: This is the only inquiry that can have a negative impact on your FICO score. When applying for new credit, you will authorize the company to run your credit report to approve it. The company will run your credit and analyze your payment history, debt load, and ability to pay back on time. This inquiry will either match to an active tradeline or not. If it matches up, that is good. If there is no matching tradeline, the computer will assume you were rejected, and it will negatively affect your score.

Current creditor: As part of your contract with a creditor, they can run your credit anytime they want to. They would do this to see why you are making late payments or to see why you have not used the card in a while. I always think that Saks runs my credit to see if I am sneaking off to Bloomingdales!

Promotional inquiries: Credit card companies buy lists of names of potential customers. "Congratulations, you have been pre-approved for a free credit card at Dale's Place!" In order to see if they want to waste the time sending this to you, they run a short credit check for informational purposes. They are allowed to do this and it does not count against you!

Self-inquiry: We are allowed to obtain a copy of our own credit report directly from each of the three credit bureaus. In fact, it is free once a year—which I will cover later in this chapter—and certainly does not count against you. Be aware of the free credit report ads, infomercials, and internet pop-up windows. Those free credit reports are probably from list service companies and are designed entice you with the free credit report to get your valuable information. The credit report is run by a third party and will count against you!

Other inquiries: An employer or insurance company might also run your credit as part of their investigation. These inquiries will not affect your score. However, I have heard of banks running a credit check to open up a new account—this will affect you.

Bankruptcies

Bankruptcy can be a credit killer and will appear on your credit report for 10 years; however, a lender will give you a mortgage again four years after the date of filing of Chapter 7, 11, or 12. A Chapter 13 (in which you arrange to pay off creditors) must be completed for two years prior to a mortgage application. There have been extenuating circumstances under which the bank will allow a borrower to obtain a mortgage after only two years. If the bankruptcy is due to a nonrecurring event beyond the borrower's control, they will look at it. Use your own imagination, as I have never been privy to this happening.

If you do declare bankruptcy, immediately after the discharge begin cleaning up your credit. It is not hard, but takes time and effort. Make a copy of your discharge letter and schedule of creditors included from the bankruptcy papers and send it to each of the three credit bureaus. Explain that you would like all of these items updated to show balance due as zero and that the debt was included in the bankruptcy. This will show that they are no longer owed and should not be considered a debt. Otherwise, they will probably show as open judgments or profit-and-loss write-offs. Again, ask for a copy of the updated report. You might have to do this a few times until it is complete. While you are at it, check for any erroneous personal information and rid yourself of old inquiries.

The key is to begin a positive credit record and good history immediately after the discharge. You can do this by taking out secure credit cards (Capital One), joint credit cards, high-interest car loans, or keeping a few existing cards open outside of the bankruptcy. To demonstrate a willingness to be responsible, the lender will look for a clean record of 24 months. The lender will require a housing expense also, so make sure you are writing checks for rent or other housing expense. I suggest four major tradelines, active and open for 24 months. This will create an excellent history and higher FICO score (660 or more).

Ask the bureaus to remove the bankruptcy from your record after 10 years. You can actually make the request after seven years; sometimes they will remove it early. It also removes anything that was included in the bankruptcy. Check your credit report twice a year after this, because sometimes the information pops back on.

Foreclosures

You can get a mortgage from FNMA five years after the foreclosure was completed by discharge or dismissal. Of course, other lenders and banks will offer you a perfectly good mortgage right after a foreclosure. If the foreclosure is less than seven years old, they will limit it to purchase loans and no cash-out refinances for primary residences only. Most lenders will require at least 10 percent down and a minimum FICO score of 680.

The lender will review your credit report through a microscope, making sure you have reestablished a minimum of four perfect tradelines, two at least from major credit cards. Most important, they want proof of your current housing situation and timely payments. So, if you are paying rent, keep those canceled checks. There cannot be more than two late payments in the previous 24 months on any credit card and zero on a housing payment. Of course, there can be no new judgments or collection accounts because you were supposed to have learned your lesson.

There are people that fall into foreclosure but are able to get out before it is too late. When people sell their homes after the foreclosure begins but before the home is sold, they could qualify for a mortgage after only two years. If there was a deed in lieu of foreclosure, where the people give the home back to bank, they might qualify for a mortgage after four years. Also, if a person sold the house for less than they owed (short sale) and the bank accepted that amount as payment in full, they could also qualify for a mortgage after four years.

In all foreclosure circumstances, the borrower must demonstrate they are financially sound and capable of paying their mortgage and bills in the future.

Judgments and Collection Accounts

You must pay off most judgments, collection accounts, and liens prior to closing. You must pay things like past-due child support and garnishments. There are some cases where the bank will let a few small and/or old judgments slide if they feel it will not impair the mortgage position or the borrower's ability to make payments. Most banks abide by the rule that if there are several judgments that total more than $5,000, all of them must be paid in full.

If you have any collections, judgments, and/or profit-and-loss write-offs, make a list of them and contact the creditors directly. Ask them to settle the account(s). When they accept, ask them to send you a letter accepting your offer before you send them your check. Send this letter to the bureaus with proof of payment, asking them to update your account and send a revised report. You can get judgments and collection accounts removed after seven years if the creditor does not renew the filing.

Note that when you call to settle an old debt, start with 50 percent and then top out at 70 percent. How much they will take depends on how long it has been out there, if the debt was sold, how many times it was sold, and if it was written off. As they say, money talks, and BS walks—so be ready to pay. You cannot bust their chops and then tell them you will pay it monthly or call them when you have the dough. The collectors will tell you to pay it by the end of the month and they will take it off your credit report that month. This is a fallacy; they will never do the work for you but will send you a letter. Send this letter out to each of the three bureaus immediately, even though it will take a while (at least 30 to 90 days) to be updated and improve your FICO score. Another falsity the collection agents will tell you is that if you settle for less than the full amount it will look terrible on your report and lower your score even more. Not true—settle.

Student Loans

Make sure that student loans show as consolidated, deferred, or paid off, because they always affect your score. If you consolidated your loans, make sure that the original lender does not also report as an open loan. Remember that default does not mean defer, because they will not give you a mortgage if you do not pay your student loans!

Identity Theft Nightmare (It Happened to Me!)

Nine million Americans have their identities stolen each year. More than half of these cases could have been avoided by consumer awareness. It is becoming a global business with the outreach of the internet.

Identity theft occurs when someone uses your identification to commit fraud or other crimes. *Financial identity theft* occurs when someone steals your identity—your name, Social Security number, or credit card(s)—and either takes out new credit or makes charges on your credit card(s).

If you are a victim of any kind of identity theft, there is a process you need to go through. First thing first: file a police report. You want the fact that you are an identity-theft victim on record so that you can show it to the credit bureaus. Contact all three credit bureaus immediately to notify them, and make sure they put a fraud alert on your report.

You should also request a credit freeze if your state allows it. A credit freeze prohibits credit from being issued in your name. You should cancel any credit cards that have been physically stolen or ones where the number may have been stolen. Let the bureaus know which accounts are closed so that they can keep an eye out for potential charges on those accounts. In addition, you will need to contact the Federal Trade Commission and fill out an identity theft form that you need to use to dispute charges made on your accounts. (Isn't this awful?) Remember to change your PINs and passwords, and shred your mail before throwing it out.

Once you've gone through this process, you can begin to restore your credit. Once you put a fraud alert on your report, you are entitled to free credit reports twice a year. Check your credit report every six months for the following problems:

- Inquiries from companies to whom you didn't give permission to run a credit check, particularly for credit cards or tradelines you didn't apply for

- High balances that aren't yours
- Any judgments that aren't yours
- Address or employers that aren't yours

With dedication and vigilance, your credit will be back on track within as few as two years.

Identity Theft Prevention

Things I do because I'm crazy:

- Change PINs and passwords every four to six months
- Close out my checking account and open a new one every 24 to 36 months
- Keep receipts and check all credit card statements for accuracy each month
- Shred *everything*—credit card statements, utility bills, free offers ...

Hats Off to Capital One!

I was a victim of financial identity theft; however, I was lucky enough to have fraud protection on my credit card. Here's how it happened.

A few years ago, I bought flowers at my local florist on a Friday afternoon and then went away for the weekend. When I returned to my office Monday morning, there was a message from Capital One to call the customer service department. I thought that was weird, so I looked at the 800 number on the back of my card and called that number. (I did not want to call the number left on my machine for fear it was a bogus number from a scam.) Capital One told me there had been an unusually high number of purchases made on my card over the weekend and wanted to ensure I had made them. It turned out there was a whopping $5,000 in charges racked up at over 30 stores in my area. (Remember, I was out of town.) I told the representative it wasn't me. I had my card with me all weekend, so how did this happen?

Apparently, there are machines (created for criminal purposes) that can be swiped with your credit card and a duplicate, identical card can be made from it. I can only assume the person who rang me up for the flowers did this and used the card fraudulently!

Capital One canceled my card, sent me a new card overnight, and had me complete a line-item report about each charge and note whether it was mine. I was not responsible for any of the fraudulent charges. This is why I hail Capital One at all my classes and to everyone I speak to about credit card theft. I reported the incident to the store but do not know what ultimately happened. I probably should have followed up, and now wish I had.

The Secured Credit Card

A secured credit card is one that is linked to a savings account for precaution. If you do not make the payments, the creditor can take the money out of your account.

Many good and bad companies provide these types of secured accounts. I would comparison shop for application fees, annual fees, interest rates, and late payments. Do not give your Social Security number or apply for a card before you have done all of your research and decided which one is the best for you. Also, please do not pay an application fee to get a credit card. It is not necessary.

The first place I would look is my own bank. If you have a savings, checking, or money market account, many banks will offer a secured credit card linked to that account. You can research online for a bank, but I would advise you to stick with a large national company that you have heard of. Capital One is pretty good. You can see I like this company.

It is important to find out if the bank reports to the credit bureaus, and to know which one(s). If they do not, don't bother. You only want a secured card from a lender that reports so you can establish history.

Rapid Rescore Response

By removing information on your credit report in certain situations, it is possible to boost your credit score rapidly—hence the name. This is legal and permanent and would be the only way to increase your score during the mortgage application process and before you close. This is an extremely useful tool now because of the FICO score ranges and the effects on interest rates.

I am not talking about the companies that advertise they can tweak your scores and get them up temporarily while you apply for a mortgage. This should be outlawed!

Only erroneous or duplicate derogatory information can be removed. A late payment, judgment, or charge-off that should be there cannot be removed. Here are some examples:

- You paid off the judgment from the hospital, but it still shows as open.
- You have a judgment from American Express that was also sent to three separate collection companies. It shows as a collection account four times, when it is really only one.
- You paid off your Sears bill, but it shows as a profit-and-loss write-off.

Your loan officer will help you work through this by analyzing the report and looking for anything that can be fixed ASAP. Items included would be judgments or collection accounts that were paid off and still show as open, or open accounts that you are able to pay off right away. As a further step, the credit service will do a free analysis and test run to see what will benefit your score and by how much. They run it through the engine to see the effects. Cool, huh?

I must stress that the analysis is a maybe and is not guaranteed. We have done everything per instructions and have seen scores go down or simply stay the same. This can really make clients mad because they used their money and paid something off that they probably did not want to. Again, this is not a sure thing, so blame the computer, not your loan officer.

Creditors must provide documentation (on their letterhead and dated within 30 days of the date you are sending the letter to the credit bureau) showing the account was paid off, erroneous, or a duplicate. Most important, the letter must state that the information will be removed from your credit report. This letter is sent to the rescore service company along with any other paperwork you have, such as canceled checks or satisfaction letters, and they update the info and rescore your FICO. This is done within 48 hours! If you did it the old-fashioned way of sending letters and waiting, it takes at least 30 days to change your score.

This feature is not necessary to update recent payoffs of accounts, but if you were doing this, I would pay down any cards that are over that 50 percent of credit limit and ask them to update it. They will do this free of charge.

This service is expensive to use and does not guarantee results. The fee can be upward of $120 per item ($20 per tradeline per credit bureau). If it is a joint account, then multiply that by two fees.

Make sure it is worth the time and effort, because results are not guaranteed. I have seen it increase scores by 20 to 40 points in some cases when the client really worked on it and had big things to change. When is it worth it? When the increased score will move you into the next FICO score level and your interest rate will be lower. Nowadays, this can be a real money saver!

You must be sure that the company that does this service is an authorized affiliate of the three credit bureaus. For example, I use a credit service called First American because I have a contract with them.

You, as a lay person, cannot go direct. You need an authorized service, not some company that you found over the Internet promising miracles.

Consumer Credit Counseling

Late-night television and drive-time radio ads will make credit counseling sound like the perfect answer to the person with too much debt or behind on their bills. Unfortunately, it can be more damaging than working it out yourself.

Credit counseling is typically a for-profit company affiliated with a not-for-profit company, guised as a consumer advocate. They will tell you that they can negotiate with your creditors for lower interest rates, reduced payment, and fees. Most credit counselors want you to have them negotiate payment plans to all of your creditors and then make one monthly payment to them to distribute for you. What the for-profit side is doing is buying the debt at a reduced amount, but collecting a higher payment from you. The profit is the difference in the payment, which is not passed on to the consumer.

Unfortunately, your credit report shows that the accounts are in consolidation or counseling. Although that might not negatively affect your FICO score, any counseling program is not looked upon fondly by mortgage lenders. They will want to see the agreements, length of time completed, and months left to go. Many lenders now think of credit counseling along the same lines as Chapter 13 and require a minimum of two years after completion before offering a new mortgage.

Also, if the company makes one late payment on your behalf, it shows up on your credit report. If you need to make payment arrangements, don't be lazy; do it directly with the creditors yourself or hire a lawyer.

College Students

If you are a college student, you may find yourself in a situation similar to individuals who are new to this country in terms of having no credit history. However, as a student you are in a better position because creditors market to you, especially during orientation week-end when they are on campus. They are just itching to get you to sign up for your first credit card. Nevertheless, watch out! They know temptation is hard for college students to resist, and many students spend more than they can easily pay back.

Before signing on, compare interest rates and fees. Do not get lured in by incentives such as double airline miles for gym members and points for cell phone payments unless you have to pay these bills any-way and there are no better incentive cards around. Shop around, look at the bank where you have your checking account, check out Bank of America and Capital One Bank, and discuss it with your parents.

Remember, spend only what you can pay off. Use credit cards to build your credit, not to start adulthood in major debt. The key is to keep a low credit limit and low balance. After a few months of timely payments, the bank will increase your credit limit. Enticing as it is, call them and tell them to lower it back to the original amount. Cut yourself off mentally at half the amount you can spend and try to pay it in full every month. If you start to go underwater, keep the card in your sock drawer for a few months until you catch up. Remember, credit is a privilege, not a luxury.

Alternative Credit Profiles

If you have no credit history and want to apply for credit, the lender will accept a nontraditional credit report. They are created by a credit-reporting agency, which your lender or loan officer can help you do.

There are different levels of nontraditional credit. The bank requires you to have at least four from the following list. There must be 12 months established and perfect payment history.

Tier I: (Four of these)

- Proof of payment for housing expense (canceled rent checks)
- Utility bills (as many as you can of: gas, electric, water, tele-phone, and cable)

Tier II (One of these)

- Medical insurance payment
- Auto insurance
- Life insurance premium payment
- Renter's insurance

Tier III (One of these)

- Payments to furniture store
- School tuition
- Child-care payments to a day care
- Payments on loan from an individual

A credit card, which you are an authorized user on, is no longer valued as credit for you. This means that if you have a friend or relative who added you on as an authorized user, this will not go onto your credit record and will not count as payment history, even if you paid the bill yourself. This is new, and killed many people's quest to begin building a credit profile. You now have to be the person who applied for the credit card and get a co-signor!

Loan Approval

If there are two borrowers, as long as one has traditional credit, the loan can be approved if …

- It is a single-family, owner-occupied primary residence.
- The transaction is for a purchase or no cash-out refinance (taking equity out of the home is not allowed).
- The borrower with traditional credit must contribute at least 50 percent of the total income.
- Both borrowers must be salaried—not self-employed.

New to America?

If you are new to this country, it is important to get a Social Security number and U.S. driver's license. If you are planning on working or living in the United States for a time, it is best to obtain credit here right away. In addition to your Social Security number and U.S. driver's license, you will need a copy of your visa and passport and proof of residence. You will have an easier time if you already have established employment and residence and hold an American Express, VISA, or Mastercard from your country of origin.

Credit Reports from Other Countries

Several other countries do some type of credit rating; however, they are not as detailed as the American report. The United Kingdom and Canada would be most similar to ours. Lenders will take a credit report from a foreign country as part of the file if the report meets the same standards. The report must be in English or translated into English. If there is a FICO score in the report, it will not be used and additional alternative credit must be supplemented in the file.

It has become more difficult for foreign nationals to buy properties by obtaining mortgages. If they cannot buy with cash, finding a lender can be an arduous project. It would be imperative for a U.S. credit profile to be provided with three credit scores. This means that credit cards and loans must be obtained here in the United States and be active for a minimum of 12 months.

Free Credit Report—For Real!

By law, you are entitled to one free copy of your report every year. Remember, you want to get your credit report directly from the source so it is not considered an "inquiry." You may obtain it from one of the three national credit bureaus or from FairIssac and Company. I have listed the most recent contact information next. You may visit the websites to learn more about FICO scores and reporting.

Equifax

www.equifax.com

Go online to get a free credit report, but you have to put your credit card information in. They sign you up for a credit score-monitoring program that is free for the first 30 days and then costs $14.95 monthly. You can cancel after the first 30 days, but I am sure you get charged at least one month.

Experian

www.experian.com

In order to get your free credit report, you have to sign up for www. annualcreditreport.com and order their credit tracking service. You must cancel within the first seven days, or you will be billed monthly.

TransUnion

www.transunion.com

This was the only one where I did not have to put in my credit card information and remember to cancel a useless monthly service.
I thought it would be best for this book if I actually went through this exercise. Actually painless, it took less than five minutes to complete and receive. The only bad thing I found here was that my opt-out option for e-mail advertisements expired after two years, and you know I will forget about it. I would also have to pay an additional $7.95 to get my FICO score. I know my FICO score, so I declined. Besides, I would have to give them my credit card info. All in all, not bad.

FairIsaac and Co.

www.myfico.com

This is not a bureau but the granddaddy of the FICO scoring system, so I thought it should be listed here. Again, they offer the free credit report but you have to pay for it. It is $15.95; however, they do give you a copy of your report, your FICO score, and a simulator to do an analysis for improvement.

The Lender Must Have an Official Tri-Merge Credit Report

One of the many questions I am asked is if a borrower may provide her own credit report or just fax one over from another lender. The answer is no. A consumer can get a copy of her credit report, but it is a simpler version prepared for informational purposes. This is perfectly fine, just not as detailed as a lender requires.

A lender uses a credit-reporting agency that has contracts with all three credit bureaus directly. The agency pulls credit reports from each of them and merges them into one report. In addition, public records, residence, employment, judgments, and all inquiries made in the past 90 days are checked.

The cost is under $20 dollars, unless extra work needs to be done such as rapid rescore, which you will learn about later in this chapter. A tri-merge credit report is good for 120 days, so don't worry that the bank will be running your credit report 100 times.

Wrap It Up!

- When was the last time you saw a copy of your credit report and got your FICO score?
- Do you need to make any changes or update info on your report?
- What can be done to increase your credit score over 720?
- Do you have inquiries on your report older than 24 months?
- Are you a co-signor for anyone who is not paying the bill directly or, if he is, he's not doing it on time?
- Have you recently established bankruptcy or had a foreclosure?
- Do you have no credit at all?
- Can you benefit from the Rapid Rescore Process?
- What is your loan to value and how great of an effect will the FICO score have on your loan amount?

Chapter 2

Income: Yeah, You Need That!

"I am living so far beyond my income that we may almost be said to be living apart."

—*E.E. Cummings*

Errol Flynn said, "My problem lies in reconciling my gross habits with my net income." Ain't that always the case!

The average housing expense allowed by lenders is less than 50 percent of gross monthly income, an increase in the average of 38 percent several years ago. This is an incredible number, because it is based on before-tax income. It does not take into consideration food, transportation, entertainment, or anything else for that matter. In 2008, the average American paid upward of 60 percent of their paycheck on housing. That does not leave much left over for shoes—I mean food.

The lender will figure out your debt-to-income qualifications for two categories: housing expense, known as the *front-end ratio*, and housing expense plus all other monthly payments, known as the *back-end ratio*.

Front-End Ratio

Your housing expense can consist of principle, interest, real estate taxes, insurance, Private Mortgage Insurance (PMI), second mortgage, maintenance (co-ops), and common charges (condominium), depending on what applies to you. This number is divided by your gross monthly income to get your front-end ratio. Note that the lender will always collect principle and interest from everybody, but will also figure in the other stuff even if you pay it directly to another entity.

Joe makes $10,000 a month before taxes. He pays $2,450 a month on his housing expense all together. His front-end ratio is 24.5 percent.

A desirable front-end ratio would look like this:

(Principle + interest + insurance + RE taxes) ÷ Gross monthly income = 33%

Joe's front-end ratio is calculated like this:

(1,200 + 600 + 150 + 500) ÷ 10,000 = 24.50%

He is fine! The question is, does Joe want to pay this amount for his house?

Back-End Ratio

Again, this is the total of your housing expense plus the rest of your monthly debt. What makes up the stuff in "All Other Payments"? Anything that shows up as a debt on your credit report, such as the following:

- Installment loan debt and credit cards (Visa, Target, The Gap, etc.)
- Auto and boat loans
- Student loans

- Alimony and/or child support
- Second homes
- Negative rental income on investment properties
- Funds borrowed from employment or retirement accounts (even if it does not show on your credit report, if it is being deducted from your paycheck, it will show on your stub)
- Co-signed or joint liabilities
- Other monthly obligations that have a payback of over 10 months

A couple things that do not count are the following:

- The money you pay back to your Mom each month
- Your cable, electric, and phone bills if those things do not show up on your credit report

Joe makes $10,000 a month. His housing expense of principle, interest, taxes, and insurance (PITI) is $2,450/month. He has a monthly car payment of $375, a student loan of $75 a month, and credit card payments of $100 a month. His total payments are $550 a month, which the bank adds to his housing expense.

A desirable back-end ratio looks like this:

(Housing expense + all other payments) ÷ Gross monthly income = 38%

Joe's back-end ratio is this:

$(2,450 + 375 + 75 + 100) \div 10,000 = 30\%$

Now, Rusty here is another story! His monthly income is $10,000. He has a monthly car loan of $475, student loans totaling $110 a month, credit card payments at $1,000 a month, and a loan against his 401(k) at $330 a month, for a total of $1,915 a month. His housing expense is $3,000 a month.

His front-end ratio is 30 percent. His back-end ratio is $4,915 ÷ $10,000, or 49.15 percent.

Rusty's back-end ratio is high—probably too high. He will have to find something cheaper, put down more money, pay off some of his debt, borrow money, or stay where he is. If he did not have so many other expenses, his housing expense would have worked out just fine.

As I said, ratios fall in the 33 to 38 percent range for most lenders and most loan products. I have seen ratios top 65 percent, although not all lenders will go this high, especially now. You will need to have excellent credit as well as a significant down payment, and some money in the bank for the banks to take this greater risk on your loan.

Compensating Factors

Lenders look at three things when determining a borrower's ability to repay the loan: credit score, gross income, and post-closing liquid assets. If one compensating factor is not so great, another might be grand and make up for it. Here are some examples:

- Your housing expense is 52 percent, but you have $500,000 in the bank after you close.
- Your housing expense is 49 percent, but you put a down payment of 30 percent on the house.
- Your back-end ratio is 56 percent, but your credit score is a 722.

So having great credit or a lot of money left over after closing can compensate for owing too much money. Having a small amount of debt can make up for having no money left over after the closing. Lenders analyze your disposable income as part of your overall financial picture as proof of how (wisely) you spend your money.

The good, the bad, and the ugly can always be improved. The bottom line is that now it is all about your FICO score and your loan-to-value (LTV). Everything else just adds a little sugar to the spice.

The More Toys You Have, the Smaller Your House

The average American lives well beyond his or her means. In fact, statistics show that the average household spends 5 percent more than they make! My Mom calls this "spending like a drunken sailor."

I understand that it is expensive just to live with the price of food and utilities noticeably going up all the time. The other stuff that we want or think we need is the killer.

The problem is that the more money you spend on cars, time-shares, and credit cards, the less you can spend on a house. The more payments you have on stuff you don't need, the less you have left over for the house with the white picket fence. So think before you spend on stuff you can do without, or knock yourself down a few levels on that car!

You do not want to kill your chances of affording the house you want because of the car you drive. Buy your home first, and then go out and buy your toys if you think (know) you can afford them, because, if you recall, the lender adds up your monthly payments for all of your monthly expenses (that show up on your credit report) and adds that to your housing expense.

The lender does not want your housing expense to be much more than a third of your gross monthly income or your total expenses to be much more than 45 percent of your total gross monthly income. Thus, if you have tons and tons of expenses like cars, boats, credit card debt, and time-shares, this is going to chew into the "all other stuff" part of the ratio and take a big bite of your housing expense.

Working Stiff

People who receive a paycheck for hourly wages or an annual salary are considered "salaried" borrowers. The bank will have you document your gross income before taxes and divide by 12 to figure your gross monthly income. You will be asked to provide 30 days of pay stubs and the last two years of W-2s. The Lender will also do a verbal verification of employment, meaning they will call your place of employment and verify that you are still working there, sometimes just a few days before the closing.

If more than 25 percent of your gross income is derived from commissions or bonus, the lender might request copies of your last two years of Federal tax returns with all of the attached schedules. The lender also will want to see your Schedule C to see if you write off job-related expenses.

The bonus or commissions must have a two-year history and proof that they will continue. Proof of same must be supplied in a letter from the employer. If the amount earned is not consistent each year, the lender might simply average them out. If the bonus or commission is decreasing, then the lender will not average at all and will probably only use the current year. It could be soon, where a bonus might not be used at all as income, especially in certain industry types.

Getting a Raise?

If you expect a raise before the closing and you think it will make a difference, let the lender know. They will ask you to get something in writing from your company and will want the first pay stub showing the increase. Each lender can use its own discretion to use the higher income or simply average your gross year-to-date income over the total months to qualify. If the bank will not use the higher income and the numbers are close, they might make an exception if the raise has been in effect for more than several months.

Second Job and Part-Time Employment

You may use income from a second or part-time job only if you have had the job at least part of the previous calendar year and can prove that you will continue the job the following year. Income from a second job can be used if you can provide a W-2 from the previous year and a current pay stub showing year-to-date income. Verbal verification cannot be the only substantiation. A seasonal job, such as retail Christmas sale, will qualify if the employer provides a letter that the job will be offered again the following year. Unfortunately, the income is averaged over the 24-month period, but it still can help you qualify!

I Am My Own Boss

You are considered self-employed if you own more than 25 percent of a company. It can be a corporation, partnership, or sole proprietor. A sole proprietor can be John Smith, self-employed person, or "Doing Business As John Smith, the Furniture Designer Extraordinaire."

The rule is that you must be self-employed for a minimum of two years. However, if it is less than two years, the lender will consider it, if you had been working in the same field and job type previously, without any gap in employment. Therefore, if you were the IT person at a large company for 10 years and then went out on your own doing IT as in independent, the bank would consider this. The lender will dig a little deeper into the probability of continued success of your business by analyzing education, experience, demand, location, and nature of business.

If you are self-employed, you will need a greater level of proof of income—more paperwork. If you show enough income on your tax returns, you can provide the lender with only your personal federal tax returns from the last two years. (They will only need the federal returns, not the state, but will want all of the schedules attached.) If your income is unclear, or if you also get additional income indirectly from your company, the lender might also ask for corporate tax returns. In addition, they will require a year-to-date profit-and-loss statement. Typically, they will allow you to prepare the P&L yourself if you sign and date it. On the other hand, you may own the company and get a paycheck. If your W-2 shows enough income, you might not need to show the lender your corporate information or even your personal tax returns. However, be prepared to provide your last two years (Federal) business tax returns anyway, because the banks are getting very strict on documentation.

The amount of documentation required depends on the lender and who is doing the looking. The lender might also ask for additional information, such as a business license or a letter from your accountant stating that you have been self-employed for X number of years and that your business is in good standing.

If the income fluctuates from year to year, the lender might average the last two years and your year-to-date net income from the P&L. However, if there is a substantial drop in income, the lender might be concerned that this is a trend downward and will need explanations as to why and guarantees of a turnaround. In most cases of declining income, the lender will qualify the mortgage based on the latest year just to be safe, and might only use the average income or explanation as a consideration.

If you are moving money from your business account to your personal account to purchase the home, you will need to document the transfers. The lender will also want a letter from your accountant stating that "you have full use of the corporate funds and taking the money out of the business account will not impair the operation of the business in any way."

Marcia is a partner in a big law firm in New York. She makes about $550,000 a year, part salary, a yearly bonus, and partner distribution. Most law partnerships hate to give the tax returns out for individual use, and I know it. First, I ask for the last two pay stubs and two years of W-2s. If the salary alone is enough to qualify for the mortgage, the lender will not ask for either the personal or the corporate tax returns. I will not have to bother the client or make copies of huge returns for the bank. If you own a company and make a salary, ask if this will be enough to qualify you before you start copying the corporate returns.

Tom the IT guy had a nice job with Borders but decided he could do better out on his own. So he left 18 months ago and started Tommy's Computer Company. The previous year's income was very good, more than he made at Borders, but the year-to-date from this year was substantially worse. The lender tried to average the income over 18 months, but it did not make sense. They asked him to explain why this year was so low, and it turned out he had a big contract that he had lost. He could not prove that he would be able to pick up replacement business so the lender rejected the loan.

The Consultant or Independent Contractor with One Employer (Not Joe the Plumber)

More and more people are employed as consultants, independent contractors, or freelancers but work almost exclusively for one company. The person is considered self-employed for tax purposes, but the lender looks at the relationship as "employed" for loan qualification and stability of employment.

If you fall into this category, you will need to show the lender your IRS Form 1099s and supply a letter from the company you work for explaining your job description, length of time, and probability of a continued work relationship.

Normally, when people are newly self-employed, they need to show two years of work history. However, if you were a long-term employee who was asked to resign due to age or for company benefit/tax purposes but stayed on as a consultant or independent contractor, the guidelines are easier. If you remain in the same job position, 12 months is enough if 6 months are included in *previous year's* tax year. For example, you resign in April 2007. You become an independent

contractor to the same company in July 2007. You apply for a mortgage in April 2008. In all cases, you will have to provide a copy of
your employment contract or a letter from your employer stating the
relationship.

Gap in Employment

A gap in employment is considered anything more than one month
between jobs. In some industries, frequent job changes are normal
and with occasional gaps in between. However, if one has a period of
several months without employment, an explanation is required. In
addition, the lender will look at the borrower's overall financial stability such as credit profile and liquidity after closing. They will also
look at job type, education, and probability of continued employment
in the field.

My favorite example is one of a friend who took a year off to spend
time with his young daughter. John had a great job with an engineering firm, traveled the world, and was paid well. He sold an investment property and was able to bank a large sum of money, enough to
live off for a year or two. He felt he was financially stable enough and
left his job in April of 2005. After traveling and enjoying his daughter's youth for some time, he took a job at another engineering firm
in September of 2007. He applied for a mortgage in March of 2008
to buy a new home. His explanation of the gap along with his financial stability and job type allowed the lender to approve the loan for
him. Although he had an almost two-year gap, he had been working
in the previous calendar year at the new job and showed continued
probability in employment. The heartfelt explanation letter also
helps, so be honest; it works much better than stories.

Rental Income

If you manage, live in, and/or are buying a multi-family house (two to
four units), the lender will use 75 percent of the gross rental income
in addition to your regular salary to qualify you.

When applying for a loan, the rental income is included in your loan application. If you are buying a new house, you will include the "proposed rental income" with your regular income. If you own the house and are doing a refinance, you will include the rent in your income section. With a refi, the lender may also ask for copies of your leases and a copy of the previous year's tax returns to show Schedule E rental income.

Most important, the lender will require additional information in the appraisal called the *Comparable Rent Schedule*. This section will show the rental income and expenses of the property, as well as comparable rental units in the area. It is similar to preparing the sales comparison (see section on appraisals in Chapter 4) to the house value. The cost of this required information will be approximately $150. Make sure it is requested with the original appraisal—not as an afterthought. That would cost you, because the appraiser will have to do additional work after he's already finished the appraisal. (Note: If there is a huge discrepancy between your numbers and the appraiser's numbers, it will also open a Pandora's Box.)

If you are an investor (not living in the property), the lender will want to see experience in property management, so you will have to prove two years of property management experience. The lender will ask for your resumé and certainly tax returns as proof. Because you are not living there, 75 percent of the *total* property rent is used in calculating income in addition to your salary. If you are a first-time investor, the lender will require a higher down payment (around 25 percent) to reduce its risk.

Investor Loans Are Harder to Come By Now

Some lenders will not even do loans for investor properties, and if they do, the loans are capped at 75 percent of the value and have higher interest rates and costs.

In other words, let's say you have a four-unit house that rents out for $1,000 per unit, totaling $4,000 for the month. The lender will add $3,000 (75 percent of the gross rents) a month to your regular salary for your total monthly income. The reduced amount allows for vacancy factors and expenses resulting from repairs and unforeseen items. If there is a negative cash flow from the rental, the amount is deducted from your salary. The issue is that most people fudge on the tax returns which will show a loss, even if they really are making a profit on the property. I guess that does not make for a very good investment!

So your salary using rental income is calculated like this:

$1,000 × 4 units = $4,000 × 0.75% = $3,000 (Net rental income) + $10,000 (Your salary) = $13,000 (Total income used to qualify)

Using Rental Income

If you *live* in a multi-family house (two to four units), the rental income from your unit will not be used.

Rental Income from Other Real Estate Owned

If you own multiple properties, the lender will definitely want your last two years of federal tax returns with the Schedule E documenting rental income and expenses. The lender will add back depreciation, interest expense, and real estate taxes. Either a profit or loss will be taken for each property.

If the rent has been increased in the current year, new leases and a copy of the canceled rent check should be provided in order to use the higher rental income.

If a rental property is not included in the tax returns, leases must be provided with canceled rental income checks. Even if you own property that has no mortgage, it must be listed on your tax returns. Because the lenders now request personal tax returns, I suggest including all properties you own on the loan application, even the swamp land in Florida your cousin convinced you to buy!

Foreign Nationals

A foreign national is a citizen and resident of another country who periodically visits the United States. Many like to have homes to live in and enjoy during their stays. A foreign national is not an American citizen, permanent resident alien, or nonpermanent resident alien. Think of it as someone who likes to come for a visit, but hates to stay in hotels!

Before 9/11, it was much easier for non-Americans to purchase real estate here. Since then, it has become a more questionable transaction, and the guidelines to borrow mortgage money are much stricter:

- The LTV can be no more than 75 percent of the purchase price.
- A tax ID number is required if the borrower does not have a U.S. Social Security number.
- Most banks will require a renewable visa or green card, even if the borrower can provide a valid U.S. Social Security number.
- The property must be a primary or second home (single family or condo).
- The source of funds to purchase the home must be from domestic or foreign bank accounts. (Cash in a suitcase is not allowed).
- The funds must be in a U.S. bank account for a minimum of 60 days before use.
- The transfer of money used for the transaction must be documented.

- The borrower must have at least six months' worth of housing expenses post-closing.

- Employment and income in the foreign country of origin must be verified.

- An international credit report will be ordered if there is no credit in the United States.

- No late payments are allowed on any tradelines, foreign or domestic. None!

- If a borrower appears to be a Politically Exposed Person (PEP),* then the file must be manually underwritten, and suspicious activity must be reported to a government agency.**

- If the borrower's country of origin is on the Non-Eligible Country list for the government's anti-money laundering program, then the transaction will be reported immediately to the authorities.**

*A Politically Exposed Person (PEP) is defined as one who has some connection to an embassy, government, or some foreign agency.

** You can assume I am telling you not to apply for a mortgage.

Trailing Borrower Income

What happens if you are transferred, and your co-borrower has not yet found a job in the new location, but you need both incomes to qualify for a mortgage? The lender will use what is called "trailing borrower" income. A trailing borrower can be anyone who has lived with the borrower before and will be living with them again. It used to be only a spouse, but then Fannie Mae decided to get real and open it up to fiancé, same-sex partner, or even a parent who will be moving and living with the borrower.

Your co-borrower must prove employment and income from a job in the location she is leaving. The lender will use up to 100 percent of the total income she earned, as long as it's not more than 33 percent of the total income needed to qualify. Does that make sense? Let me provide an example.

Fred and his Mom are moving to Phoenix. Fred is the primary borrower, but they still need the Mom's income to qualify. Mom works as a hotel manager in Albany, New York, making $36,000 a year. She can find a similar job with the same income once she gets to Phoenix. Fred makes $3,000 a month, but they need to show $4,000 a month to qualify for the loan. They can use $1,000 a month for the mother's potential income and it will be 25 percent of the total needed. So the numbers work.

Other requirements include the following:

- The mortgage may only be for an owner-occupied primary residence (no second homes).
- The co-borrower must prove two years of continuous employment in the old location.
- The co-borrower must provide a statement of intent that he will seek employment in the new location.
- The job market and salaries in the new location must be comparable to the old one (the lender will check online employment/income sites).
- You must have six months of housing expenses left over after closing, just in case the co-borrower does not get a job right away.
- You should have a FICO score of 680 or higher.

Trailing Borrower Note

Your trailing borrower cannot be self-employed. Why wouldn't he be taking the business along if he could?

Weird and Different Income

Not everyone makes money the conventional way—by working. There are other types of income that may qualify the borrower completely or in addition to ordinary income.

- *Interest and dividends:* A two-year average is used to figure interest and dividends. The principle used to generate the income must be available after the closing and remain in the accounts to continue generating income. It cannot be a one-shot deal or a huge windfall on a stock tip; there has to be some history.

- *Notes receivable:* If you hold a personal note and are collecting interest for a minimum of one year back and three years forward, the interest may be added in as income. If you hold a mortgage on a house or a note on a business, the payments collected may be used. However, if your brother owes you $10,000 and pays you $100 a month in cash, you cannot use it.

- *Trust income:* If the trust is irrevocable and guarantees a payout for three years after closing, the income may be used. You'll have to provide a copy of the trust agreement and proof of the previous two years of payments.

- *Capital gains:* A borrower may use capital gains income from the sale of publicly traded stock or real estate if this is typical income for her. In other words, if you have stock and sell it to make a profit, buy another stock and sell it to make profit, etc., you can use the profit as income. You must prove that you have done this for at least three years by showing your tax returns, as well as be able to forecast that there will be additional gains for the following three years. In addition, you must maintain the same value of the original asset throughout the time period. A three-year average of net profits will be used to figure income.

- *Stock options:* Stock options are a way that big-shots get paid at big publicly traded companies. It is simply receiving an option to purchase stock at a certain price in lieu of getting paid salary. These can be used as income if there is a history of exercising these options and proof of the quantity of options available and the price and the schedule for vesting. An average will be used to qualify for income purposes.

- *Retirement income and pension:* Income from IRAs, 401(k)s, pensions, and the like is used as if it is regular income. Remember, this income is not taxed, so the lender will increase it by 125 percent to calculate your income! The lender will ask for proof of continued payments as well as tax returns. They will take a harder look at your liquid assets and may require a larger down payment. If the payout is a one-shot deal, it cannot be used. Furthermore, if a portion of the principle is being used to purchase the house, a percentage of the income will be reduced accordingly. Please know it is illegal for lenders to discriminate against age, so it does not matter how old the borrower is.

- *Social Security, disability, and public assistance:* This income must be verified as nontaxable. You'll be required to provide documentation and tax returns. You must also show proof that it's likely to continue for a minimum of three years. *Temporary, partial, or permanent disability all qualify.*

- *Unemployment income:* You can use this income if you're a seasonal worker, such as a landscaper or tradesperson. You'll have to prove that you received unemployment for at least two previous years. An average will be taken from the tax returns. *Proof is imperative, so get together your records of payments received.*

- *Alimony and child support:* You must show you have received alimony and/or child support for a minimum of six months and prove it will continue for three years. You will only have to provide limited documentation due to privacy restrictions.

- *Foreign income:* You will have to show proof of income; the lender will determine the currency exchange rate. If you have investment income, rental income, or self-employment income reported in another country, it could be used as income. Non-Permanent Resident Aliens may not use foreign income to purchase property in the United States. If you are getting a high interest return on your secret Swiss bank account, leave it off the loan application.

- *Working for family owned business:* This income may be used, but the lender will perform an extra layer of review. The lender will ask for the last two years of tax returns, W-2s, and verbal verification of employment and job status. The lender might request proof of company ownership to make sure the borrower is really not self-employed.

- *Foster care:* You'll have to show proof from an agency that you've received income from being a foster care provider for a minimum of 12 months and that you'll likely continue. Income is limited to a baker's dozen of children—kidding!

- *Boarder income:* This income may be used if a "relative" has lived with you for at least 12 months and pays rent, can provide proof of residency (license, passport, etc.) and provide 12 months of canceled checks. A relative is defined as a blood or adoption relative, fiancé, domestic partner, or anybody you are closely related to or sleeping with. Boarder income can be no more than 30 percent of the total income needed to qualify for the loan. Not all lenders or loan programs allow this income to be used, so check with your loan officer first.

- *Lottery for life:* This is my personal favorite. A friend of mine won $1,000 a week for life, gave up her job in New York City, and moved to Florida. She bought a little condo on the beach in Miami, and there she happily resides. (All she had to do was show documentation from the Lottery Commission and it was like a paycheck!)

Buying a New Car Before You Close Is a No-No

I don't know why, but before people are closing on their new home, they either go on a big trip or buy a new car. (FYI, it is always polite to tell your loan officer that you are disappearing for a week or two in case she needs something crucial.) I am always pleased when a client calls and asks if he should buy the car before he closes. My answer is this: pick out the car, get the deal tied up, and wait until after the closing.

In addition, if you have less than 8 months left on a car loan or 10 months left on a lease, the lender does not add the payment into your ratio. However, on a lease, you must prove you are buying out the lease at the end of the term and have the funds to do so. If you buy/lease a new car before the closing, the payment is calculated into the back-end ratio. This can change your numbers and lower the mortgage amount you qualify for. Depending on the car payment, it can increase your debt ratio 3 to 10 percent or just enough so that you do not qualify for the mortgage. Also, credit inquiries made by car dealers could lower your FICO score. So wait!

My Business Pays My Car Payments

Remember, if the debt shows up on your personal credit report, it's included in your liability, unless proven otherwise. FNMA guidelines enable you to have this debt eliminated by producing canceled checks from the business showing it comes out of the business funds. The lender might also ask for business tax returns showing the business takes that expense. Note that if the account shows a history of being late, it will be included in your personal debt.

I've had many self-employed clients who rack up huge monthly bills on their personal side but pay them (legitimately) through their businesses. If a business pays the owners' car payment, it may be excluded when calculated the personal debt. These include big-ticket items such as cars, equipment leases, and credit cards. Large purchases that appear more as luxuries, such as a boat, second home, time-share, or multiple cars usually don't fly.

If you are salaried and receive a car allowance, it can be considered income; however, all related expenses (car leases/payments) must be included in your liabilities. Proof of car allowance paid and reported on W-2 must be documented as well as the car payment.

Co-Signing for Someone Else's Debt Lowers Your Borrowing Power

Unless it's clearly documented that the other signor is making timely payments for a minimum of 12 months (or the whole time, whichever is less), the lender will consider the debt to be yours. Therefore, make sure those you're helping also help you. They will need to provide you with proof of payments for the lender. Proof can be canceled checks or receipts from automatic deductions from a bank account. If there are late payments, then the debt still will be counted as yours because those you have co-signed for are not acting responsibly. So make sure they make the payments out of their accounts and on time. The lenders are tightening up on this and are now requiring that the account be held jointly and not just being paid by another person. This is especially true for mortgage payments that one person co-signs for another; they are still responsible in case of default.

Do not let them give you cash and have you make the payments. You cannot prove they gave you the cash. This setup is one of the biggest financial mistakes parents tend to make when helping a child. Usually they are covering because their child does not make payments on time, doesn't save enough of her earnings, or simply doesn't pay. Big mistake! It's better to teach your loved ones to be financially responsible.

Now, there is a legal snafu in some situations: if you're *jointly* liable with someone, and you both make the payments, the entire debt will be counted as yours, even if it's really the other person's debt and he made all the payments. *You're jointly liable if you're a husband and a wife, but not if you're an aunt and a nephew.* You cannot lie about this—there's coding in your credit report that defines the relationship, and by law spouses are financially liable for each other's debt. As I advise all my clients, when a divorce is imminent, cut up the cards and get your own!

Didn't Sell Your House Yet and Need to Close on the New One?

Selling your current home and buying a new one at the same time can be a stressful and sticky situation if you haven't sold the old home before you have to purchase the new home. Of course, the best scenario is to close on the sale in the morning, take that money in certified funds, and close on your new purchase in the afternoon. It is hard to believe, but with a good team in place, this often happens. However, sometimes it does not. Here are three situations and three resolutions:

1. Your income is enough to cover the housing expense for the new and current home simultaneously. Some people can afford two homes at once, and they don't all live in Hollywood. The lender will calculate your housing expense ratio for the new house and add the current housing expense into your back-end (total monthly debt) ratio. The back end might be a little high, but the lender knows it's a temporary situation, so it will give a little leeway. The lender prefers when you have great credit and are putting down 20 percent or more.

2. You are closing on the sale within a few weeks, but you have to purchase the new house now. The lender will ask for fully executed contracts for the sale of your home, a "clear to close" commitment letter from your buyer, and a letter from your attorney stating the confirmed closing date with an explanation for the delay. Lenders do not really like this

situation, because anything can happen between now and then, such as death, divorce, or property destruction, and the deal can go south. The lender will accommodate if it appears that all is well and you have compensating factors, such as enough money in the bank to cover both payments for a while if you have to.

3.   You are keeping the old house and renting it out. You might decide to keep your current house as an investment property and not sell it. This could be for any number of reasons, such as you cannot sell it because the market is bad or you owe too much on it. In fact, you might want to keep it with the idea of using it as a second home later on, or it is simply a good investment. Whatever your reason might be, the lenders have heavy requirements for this situation.

If the loan for the new house is under 70 percent of the purchase price, then the lender will allow 75 percent of the rental income to be used as income. In turn, the lender will include 100 percent of the housing expense in the borrower's debt. A rental-market analysis showing proof of true market rents is required. The lender will also ask for a fully executed lease, copies of cleared security, and rental checks from the tenant.

If the loan for the new house is greater than 70 percent of the purchase price, the lender will not allow any rental income to be used and will require six months of payments for both housing expenses to be in reserve!

If you are keeping the house as a second home, you will need to qualify for both loans and have an additional six months of payments in reserves.

Wrap It Up

- Before getting started, have your paperwork in order. For salaried borrowers, have last 30 days of pay stubs, W-2s, and your Federal tax returns ready if requested. Have any other paperwork documenting commission, bonus, or special circumstances together.

- For self-employed borrowers, have your proof of self-employment and the last two years of federal tax returns, both personal and business.

- If you own other properties, then have the mortgage and expense info together, leases, and tax returns.

- If you have co-signed for someone else's debt, then get a copy of the loan statement and last six months of canceled checks proving he makes the payments.

- If you have large debts for credit cards, cars, or other things that you are thinking of paying off, do so before you apply for a loan. It takes 30 to 60 days for payments to show up on a credit report and thus not be included in your debt ratios.

- If someone else or a business pays a loan for you, get the documentation so it will not be included in your monthly debt.

- If you have "weird income," get copies of statements or payments received for the last two years and proof that it continues for the next three years.

- If you are renting out your home and moving to the new one, start looking for a tenant. Lately, banks have been asking for notarized leases and copies of canceled security deposit checks.

- Be prepared! Lenders like complete loan application packages, and it makes the process go smoother for you, too!

Chapter 3

Money Matters

> "Show me the money!"
> —*Tom Cruise as Jerry McGuire*

As we know, money does not grow on trees, nor does the party last forever! We live in a *now* society where we want it now, and will worry about paying for it later. The banks believed in that as well, only asking for you to have a few dollars left in the bank after to you bought your McMansion. Well, those days are gone, and real money matters now.

Cash Reserves Are Just as Important as FICO Scores!

The rules have changed as far as money and how much you have—or don't have. Borrowers used to need only to show just enough money to close; now they need to show more than enough.

Old mortgage guidelines required only your down payment, closing costs, and two months' housing payments in reserve after you closed. The new rules require a larger down payment, closing costs, and 6 to 12 months' payments in post-closing reserves.

The more reserves you have left over after the closing, the better able you are to continue making payments if you lose your job or run into financial trouble. The lenders now also look at total debt versus liquidity. Thus, if you owe $25,000 on credit cards and have $40,000 in the bank, you could pay them all off if you had to. I used to ask borrowers to verify only enough money to make the deal work. Now I say "show me the money" and ask them for every account they have.

Liquid Assets Are Money

The true way to calculate wealth is by calculating net worth. Net worth is all of one's assets less all liabilities. For mortgage purposes, assets are any "liquid" assets or an asset that can be converted to money quickly. Therefore, government bonds are considered liquid because they can be cashed in, but a boat is not because it must be sold.

Liquid assets include the following:

- Savings and checking accounts
- Bonds
- Certificate of Deposit (CD)
- Gifts from family members that do not need to be repaid
- Money market funds
- Mutual funds
- Sale of proceeds from another house (verified)
- Retirement accounts (401(k), 403B, SEP IRA)
- Stocks
- Trust accounts
- Cash value of life insurance (verified)
- Seller-/other party-paid closing costs

The accounts do not need to be liquid to be considered an asset. Only the money needed to close the deal should be liquid. Thus, if you have $50,000 in IBM stock, it is an asset for reserves but does not need to be cashed in unless needed for the closing.

Money You Need vs. What You Have

To purchase a home, you need to show that 5 percent of the down payment came from your own money. The rest of the down payment may come from elsewhere as discussed later in the chapter. The lender will ask for proof of the down payment in the form of a cleared check from your bank. They will not allow a letter from the seller stating that they have the money just in case you are in cahoots.

In addition, the lender will require the estimated closing costs be available at the closing, including all fees and reserves for taxes, insurance, and interest. These figures are given to you in the beginning of the mortgage process and finalized prior to the closing. Depending on what type of transaction you are doing and how risky you are, the lender will require 6 to 12 months of housing payments in the bank after you close.

If you are refinancing a mortgage, all the closing costs and interest and tax reserves can be taken out of the new mortgage proceeds. However, the cash reserves required for housing expenses must come from savings.

Borrowing Against Your Retirement Plan

Retirement plans—IRAs, 401(k)s, and SEPs—can be cash-and-carry assets. You can withdraw funds or borrow (against) them and use the money as a down payment, for closing costs, or for reserves (in which case you do not have to actually cash them in).

While these accounts are entirely your money, except for Roth IRAs, they are pre-tax dollars meant for retirement, so if you withdraw funds early, you will have to pay taxes and penalties on the amount withdrawn if you are not at least 59½ years old. However, if you are a first-time homebuyer, you can withdraw up to $10,000 as an individual taxpayer and $20,000 as a married couple without incurring penalties, although you may have to pay income taxes. You must use the funds within 120 days of receiving them. The lender will require evidence of the withdrawal and deposit into your nonretirement checking or savings account.

Instead of withdrawing funds, you can opt to borrow against your 401(k) account(s) and pay it back, usually at an interest rate of prime plus 1 percent. (You cannot borrow against your IRAs.) In this case, there is no tax or penalty for early withdraw, nor are there any qualifications for borrowing, except that the amount you borrow from a 401(k) is limited to half your vested balance. A vested interest is the percentage of the total amount you are entitled to withdraw or borrow against and increases each year. You will have to provide documentation of the loan agreement and payment terms to the lender, of course. The payback period is typically four years, and your employer will deduct your payments from your paychecks. Your total monthly payment will be a debt and, as such, calculated into your ratios.

Some lender guidelines state that if you have enough money left in your 401(k) to pay back the entire amount borrowed, then your monthly payments will not be considered in qualifying for the loan. However, the new rules for mortgages require the banks to include the monthly payment for a 401(k) loan regardless. Thus, if you borrow $30,000 at $250/month and there's $30,000 still left in your 401(k) account, the lender will not calculate your monthly $250 payment. Check with your loan officer to understand how your lender calculates the payments—if he does not know, have him check and get back to you. This can make or break your ratios. Therefore, when you borrow against your 401(k) or any brokerage account, the money will become an asset but will also become a debt, assuming you want to pay yourself back.

While you lose out forever on the tax-free growth or earnings when you sell your home, the equity is tax free up to a point (check with the IRS for the current amount), so borrowing against your retirement may be a good option for first-time buyers.

Nonetheless, I find using your 401(k) or other savings plan is a big decision to make. This is hard-earned money that you're supposed to be socking away for retirement. So think long and hard before you take it out. Call human resources or the fund representative and get the details on the process and your monthly payments. Also, check with your tax advisor on the latest IRS rules. Knowing the facts in advance makes the decision process easier and less stressful.

When Is a Loan from My Father-In-Law a Gift?

A gift is considered an asset if you get it from a blood relative, legal guardian, married partner, domestic partner, or fiancé, or from a church or nonprofit organization, and don't have to pay it back.

The gift must be documented prior to the closing and presented with supporting evidence to the lender, so don't go to the closing with a bag of cash and say Aunt Marian gave you this money and you don't need to pay it back. What you need to do is provide the following items to the lender:

- Proof of transfer to you, such as copy of wire or canceled check
- A copy of deposit slip used to deposit the gift into your account
- Proof the money is in your account
- A completed affidavit (provided by lender) stating the name and address of the donor, the relationship with the borrower, address of property to be purchased, the amount of gift, and that it does not need to be paid back

Some lenders might ask for a bank statement showing the money in the donor's account, especially if it is going to be gifted at closing. The most important thing about a gift is that you don't need to pay it back, because otherwise it would be a loan and figured into your monthly debt.

Note that you'll need to contribute at least 5 percent of the purchase price for the down payment, unless the gift is for more than 20 percent of the purchase price. If the loan-to-value (LTV) is under 80 percent, then the whole down payment may be a gift.

For example, Zachary is buying a house in Washington, D.C., for $400,000. If he was taking a loan for 80 percent of the purchase price ($320,000), he would have to come up with 5 percent of his own money ($20,000) and could get a gift from his Aunt Dale for $60,000. If he was putting down 30 percent of the purchase price ($120,000), then the entire down payment can be a gift. He would still have to show closing costs and reserves.

The Use of Gifts Is Limited

You may no longer use a gift for investment properties and only occasionally for second homes. A gift of equity may only be used for a primary residence.

Gift of Equity

This occurs when a family member sells another family member her home and gives part of the purchase price as a gift. A gift of equity can only apply to a purchase of a primary residence. It cannot be a second home or investment property. The sales contract must state the full purchase price and the amount of the gift. The appraisal must reflect the gift and ensure that the house is valued at the full purchase price.

For example, Aunt Bea wants to sell her niece Pamela her home in New Jersey and move to Florida. The house is worth $350,000, but Aunt Bea will sell it to her loving niece for $300,000. The sale price for the contract is $350,000. The down payment as listed on the contract is $50,000 "as a gift of equity."

The contract price is $350,000 and the house appraises for $350,000, therefore the mortgage is based on that amount. Pamela wants a mortgage for 80 percent LTV, which is $280,000. Pam only needs to come up with $20,000 more to pay Aunt Bea her price, plus she has to pay closing costs and have a few months' worth of payments.

Pam has the $20,000 in her savings account but does not have the estimated $10,000 she needs for the closing costs and the reserves. In addition to a gift of equity, the seller in this situation may also gift money for closing costs. Be advised that some lenders will not allow this or might have their own rules, so to prevent a catastrophe at closing, make sure you tell everyone involved in the lending process from the get-go how the deal is being structured, and document everything.

Aunt Bea gives Pamela the $10,000 she needs, in the form of a cash gift (money she does not need to pay back is considered an asset). Pam is able to buy her Aunt's house for $20,000 out of pocket.

Closing Costs Paid by Seller or Other Party

Closing costs normally required to be paid for by the borrower may be paid for by the seller, builder, realtor, company relocation office, or other interested party. Most often, it is the seller paying the closing costs and is never allowed to be the lender. This contribution to closing costs is considered a finance concession and deemed an asset as if it were cash. Think of it as Monopoly money, because it is a paper debit and credit on the purchase closing statement, and never really passes hands. The concession can be no more than the actual dollar amount of the closing costs.

You can use a finance concession when buying a home whether as owner-occupied, second home, or investor-owned. This is typically negotiated in the beginning with the realtor playing a big part. The attorney rarely gets involved in negotiating concessions but must know about it when preparing the contracts.

The amount the party pays can be anywhere from 3 percent to 6 percent of the purchase price or appraised value, whichever is less, depending on the LTV of the mortgage. LTV is simply a ratio representing the amount of financing you are requesting. Therefore, if you put 10 percent down, your LTV ratio would equal 90 percent.

The following shows how much in seller concessions you are allowed to receive from the seller based on your LTV:

Seller-Paid Closing Costs

LTV		Concession
Over 90%	(primary only)	3%
75%–90%	(primary/second home)	6%
Under 75%	(primary/second home)	9%
Investment property	up to 90%	2% (regardless of LTV)

The concession must meet the following requirements to be valid:

- Written into contract of sale as a dollar amount or percent of sale price
- Reflected in the appraised value (which must equal the actual purchase price plus the concession)
- Included in the closing statement by the lender

If the amount of the concession is higher than the allowable percentage, then that portion is considered a purchase concession and will be deducted from the sale price. If the appraised value is less than the price plus concession amount, then the concession will go off the lower value. This is always hard to explain, so let me provide an example.

$300,000 \times 0.90\% = \$270,000$

6% seller concession = $18,000

$300,000 + $18,000 = $318,000 (New purchase price/appraised value)

$318,000 \times 0.90\% = \$286,200$ (New loan amount)

Rent with Option to Buy

Good timing may bring a nice deal for both tenant and landlord. The property owner will not have to use a realtor and formal negotiations, and the tenant won't have to move! For these conveniences and money savers, the property owner might negotiate a better price than he would with strangers.

The lender will allow only a portion of the rent paid over and above the "fair market rental value." The lender typically determines that amount by using an appraiser to do a rental analysis to see what the actual rent would have been over the period you rented the property. The down payment contribution is the actual rent paid less fair market rent. If the amount is negative, no portion of the rent will be allowed.

For example, Jack has been renting a house from Jill at $1,600 a month for the last two years. Jill says that Jack can apply the last 12 months of rent toward the down payment as part of the deal. This would equal $18,000. They tell the lawyer what they are doing, and the lawyer writes it into the contract that $18,000 was paid as a down payment. The lender orders the appraisal and requires a rental market analysis to be done to determine what the rent should be. The fair market rental value of the house comes back at $1,500 month. Therefore, only $100 dollars a month will be used toward the down payment. This means Jack will only get a credit for $1,200 bucks, which does him no good.

If Jack tries to fudge the numbers and says he has been paying $2,500 a month, the lender will ask to see a copy of the fully executed lease and the last 12 months of canceled checks. If Jack and Jill say they do not have copies of them, then the down payment won't apply at all. The banks are always onto the latest scheme!

Bridge Loan

When you have not sold your current residence and need to close on the new home, it is possible to get a "bridge" loan. Simply, you get a loan on your current home and pay for the new house while you wait for the sale to finalize. My parent's generation would call this a "swing" loan, which I think sounds more fun!

The requirements are as follows:

- The borrower must be able to qualify to make both housing payments, along with all other obligations.

- The loan cannot be collateralized by the old and new house (this is called a blanket mortgage).

- When the current home is sold, the bridge loan must be paid in full.

These loans are difficult to come by nowadays, given the risk involved. Perhaps obtaining a home equity loan on the current house might be easier. For this, I suggest getting the home equity loan before the house is even put on the market for sale. If a house is listed, the appraiser will indicate as such in the home-equity loan appraisal. Lenders prefer not to invest in mortgaging that they know will be paid off shortly. The lender will be very stringent with qualifying the borrower for the new loan and would insist on excellent credit as well as other compensating factors.

The Payment Abatement Program (Buyer's Bonus Program)

Another type of finance concession is where the seller makes mortgage payments for the buyer for up to the first six months.

The payments may only be for principle and interest and must be for the entire month's amount, not partial. The buyer must still pay her own taxes and insurance and must allow the lender to hold them in escrow and pay them on her behalf.

The Payment Abatement Program is restricted to purchases of single-family homes, condos (includes conversions), and townhomes. As with other types of seller concessions, the deal must be stated in the contract, noted in the appraisal, and disclosed to the lender in the beginning of the process. Some lenders have their own layer of restrictions with this program or simply do not allow it all. Therefore, check first and make sure they know and that you are following the lender's guidelines.

Again, this program is more popular with builders and developers as incentive to sell units in advance. It is a great advertising tool when markets get soft. It is also a great negotiating tool for a buyer. Be aware: the expense to the seller could be hidden in the purchase price, so make sure you are not overpaying.

Wrap It Up

- Make a list of every account you have, even if you cannot touch the money.
- Are you getting a gift from a family member?
- If you are applying rental payments toward buying a home, gather the last 12 months of canceled checks and copy of your lease with option to buy.
- Is the seller or another third party contributing toward the sale price or closing costs?

- Are you borrowing money against a savings plan? If so, make an appointment to discuss the terms and processing of the loan.

- If the seller is paying some of your closing costs, make sure everybody knows.

- How much money will you need after the closing for reserves, repairs, moving expenses, and a few months of payments?

Chapter 4

A Good Look at the Property

Nobody wants you to pay too much for your new home (other than the seller and the realtor), so you get an appraisal before you buy the home. The appraisal determines the market value of a home based on comparing its size and style with other homes in the area. Typically, it shows three other properties within 1 mile of the subject property that have sold in the last three months. Of course, there are exceptions to the rules and the appraiser has guidelines to widen the scope of the comparisons.

Nonetheless, appraisals are done by an independent licensed person who is hired by the lender. The lender requires an appraisal to be completed for all purchase as well as refinance mortgages. They use this to determine the loan-to-value (LTV) for your mortgage.

Home Value

Even if you are lucky enough to pay cash for the house, please get an appraisal to make sure the value is at least the contract price.

There Are Many Benefits to the Appraisal

An appraisal will tell you many things other than the value of the home. The form can be 10 to 15 pages chock-full of important and useful information such as the following:

- Neighborhood information
- How long the average home in the neighborhood takes to sell
- The materials the home is made of
- Heating and other utility systems used
- Square footage and layout of the rooms
- If the basement is actually usable square footage
- If there is any noticeable damage that needs to be repaired
- The last sale date and price for the home—what the seller paid for it
- Pretty pictures of the inside and outside of the home
- The replacement value of the home, which you need for insurance

It will also tell you what a few of your new neighbors paid for their homes and when.

Lender's Examination of an Appraisal

The lender will examine the entire report with a fine-tooth comb, but it mainly looks at the value of the home to determine the appropriate loan amount and how long it will take to resell it in case of foreclosure.

Determining the Loan-to-Value

The lender determines the LTV of a home using the appraisal. In a purchase transaction, the mortgage amount is based on the contract price or appraised value, whichever is lower. In a refinance, the mortgage is capped at the required LTV of the appraisal. So in getting an appraisal, you want to make sure it is worth the sale price when buying, or what you need it to be to get your refinance mortgage.

For example, Reba is buying a home for $525,000. She is getting an 80 percent LTV mortgage. Here are two scenarios:

Scenario 1

Appraised value: $575,000

Loan amount 80% LTV: $420,000 (based on purchase price)

Scenario 2

Appraised value: $500,000

Loan amount 80% LTV: $400,000 (based on appraised value)

In the second scenario, Reba will need to come up with an additional $20,000 of her own funds at the closing.

Of course, some people get a better deal than others. If you think you are getting a steal and the appraisal comes in at the exact contract price, it still might be worth way more. However, lenders will not accept appraisals that are far more than the contract price because they think there is something wrong or the buyer and seller are in cahoots. They like to see it no more than a few thousand dollars higher and a maximum 10 percent higher than the purchase price.

The lender might have questions about the appraisal, and they will contact the appraiser directly for answers. If the lender has too many questions, they might ask for a second appraisal to be done in order to compare them and ensure the value and information is correct. The lender could still reject the entire appraisal and require that they order their own new appraisal.

Of course, the borrower bears the expense of all these additional appraisals. If the chances are dimming with the lender, perhaps a new lender should be approached. I always found it amazing how one lender could reject an appraisal but another would not have one question with it! This is because they are actually reviewed by humans, and they look for mistakes to prove their worth.

It is very difficult to get an appraisal transferred from one lender to another. Although you pay for it and it is rightfully yours, the lender controls the appraisal. Assume you will have to get a new appraisal and that you will pay for it all over again. Do not be cheap and wait to save a couple of bucks. If the deal is not going right, move on!

Protecting Yourself in the Contract

If the sales price is actually lower than the true value, you certainly do not want to pay more than you should. This will show in the appraisal. However, you also want to be protected in the sales contract if this should happen.

A Mortgage Contingency Clause should be written into every contract, regardless of how badly you want the house or how sure you are to get the appropriate financing. The clause has two parts to it.

Mortgage Loan-to-Value

As stated, the LTV of a mortgage is based on the contract price or the appraised value, whichever is less.

The first part states you have X number of days to obtain a mortgage in the amount of X. The basics are that you, the buyer, will make every good-faith effort to get a mortgage, typically within 45 days. The dollar amount is based on the decided LTV of the purchase price. If you use every effort, but cannot get the mortgage, you will get your down payment back. If you waive this right, and do not get a mortgage, you lose your down payment. One should never waive this right unless they have the cash to pay for the house in full or another back-up plan (rich parents).

The second part of a mortgage contingency clause is the LTV. The clause should include the language that the appraised value should match the sales price in order for the LTV to be correctly calculated. If the appraisal comes in lower than the price, you cannot possibly get a mortgage for the correct amount. If this should happen, the seller should be asked to negotiate and lower the price. The negotiations will go as smoothly as possible depending on how badly you both want the deal to go through. If a deal cannot be made, at least you have an out and can get your money back.

Waiving a Mortgage

Just know that if you choose to waive the right and time to get a mortgage, make sure the appraised value language remains in the sales contract.

Illegal Apartments Are Bad Karma

In urban areas, single-family homes that were once affordable became expensive to maintain and were divided into units for rental income. If the work was done without the town's notification and approval, the units are probably illegal. An apartment in the basement of a house without outside access is probably illegal.

A shady realtor will tell the seller that he can market the house as a two-family house and set a price based on that. The realtor will then tell the buyer that it is a two-family house with rental income to help with the mortgage. The appraiser will check out the house status with the town records and see that it is a legal one-family and appraise it as such. It will also be noted that there is an illegal apartment in the house. When the lender sees this appraisal, the loan will be rejected immediately.

A smart and shady realtor will tell the seller she can get more for the house because there is an illegal apartment in the home. They will then tell the buyer that there is an illegal apartment, which will bring in additional income and the house is worth paying a premium for. Before the appraiser visits the house, the realtor will have the stove removed from the illegal apartment and make it look like a finished area of the house. A stove makes a home, so if it is not there, the illegal apartment becomes a "finished basement." So no one is wise to the deal and the bank will get a valid appraisal for a one-family house with a finished basement.

I have two things for you to consider. The house has to be appraised to include the premium you are paying for the extra unit, and it is illegal. An illegal unit is not covered by homeowner's insurance. If something should happen to person or property, you will not be insured and will have a huge problem on your hands. It's a problem that would never be worth the extra money you are bringing in with the illegal rents.

Second Kitchens Are Okay

This is called a summer kitchen. After World War II, there were many houses built to accommodate large families. They typically had no air conditioning, and the kitchens got very hot in the summer. Families built kitchens in the basements or lower areas with access to the outside to use for summer cooking or even as a second facility when needed. Having a summer kitchen is acceptable to most lenders and is noted in the appraisal—the appraisal should refer to it as "usual and customary." If this is normal in the area, the lender will be okay, and you will not have to remove the kitchen. This is different from an illegal apartment in the basement, which is a complete no-no.

Parking Spots and Furniture Are Not Included in Home Values

Often, a builder will offer additional items to purchase with new construction condominiums or townhouses such as parking spots and storage facilities on premises. In urban areas, these are gold to the buyer and a fabulous sales tool for the seller.

However, anything that is not attached to the real estate is not part of it and therefore not included in the value. Thus, these items may not be included in the appraised value or the mortgage. When extra items such as these are purchased with the real estate, the seller will include them in the sales contract as part of the transaction. However, the appraiser must subtract the value off the top for mortgage purposes, thus reducing the price as well as the loan amount.

The same goes with furniture and other items such as chandeliers, pool tables, and landscaping equipment. Things the seller does not need in the new home, or cannot move, might be of great value to the buyer. When personal property is purchased, it is separate from the real estate and should be treated as such for the mortgage. These items should be listed, photographed, and inspected before the closing. The items are given a value and the list is made part of the contract. If there is very little value, then that should be stated as such.

So because you cannot include this personal property in the value for the mortgage, you'll need to come up with the cash to pay for it. A crafty seller or realtor will include the price of these extras in the total sale price, but have a separate document outlining the terms, so beware.

Condominiums and Co-Ops Require More Information

When buying a condominium or co-operative apartment, you are buying a piece of a company, managed by someone else. Therefore, the lender wants to see that the building and their management are a sound investment.

The appraiser will include an additional section providing information for the following:

- Number of units sold versus unsold or empty
- Number of owner-occupied apartments versus rented out
- Whether the building is completely finished

- Whether there is a mortgage on the building that is not too big and being paid on time
- Whether the building is financially secure and has a slush fund in reserve

Fraudulent Appraisals and the Lending Process

The problem is that an appraisal is an opinion based on subjective research done by one person. The value can vary from person to person and therefore is somewhat arbitrary. The quandary is compounded by the fact that the appraisal industry had been booming, and many people started new careers thinking they could earn big bucks on sheer volume alone. Appraisers were hiring inexperienced people to do the actual inspections and never visited the homes themselves. Then they hired other inexperienced people to do the research and would not always review it as carefully as they should have. Business was booming and they had to keep up with the volume and turn-around time. Mortgage companies and realtors would drop them in a minute if they couldn't turn the work around in a matter of days. A rush was considered same-day turnaround. The '90s were a crazy time, and everybody wanted a piece of the action.

Lenders, also hiring green people off the street, could not properly train the staff to read and review the appraisals. Therefore, the under-writers were just rubber-stamping them to get through all the files.

This whole situation led to enormous manipulation in house prices. The housing industry catapulted quickly to falsely inflated values, creating phantom wealth for many people. In turn, the home equity loan became a great tool for people to remove this equity and purchase needless luxury items. You cannot tell me that something that was worth $250,000 in 2004 was worth $400,000 in 2006. It is impossible and unreasonable. Then the market began to lose steam, and inventory began to build. As more homes stayed on the market, buyers had more to choose from and could question prices.

Values were easily inflated during the real estate boom, which in turn enlarged loan amounts much higher than they should have been. As values decrease, appraisals are coming in lower, and loans are going upside down. When a loan is upside down, the borrower owes more than the home is worth. These situations will impede refinancing as well as selling. Unless the buyers must sell and can make up the difference out of pocket, they stay put.

Sales History of a Home

As part of the appraisal, the last five years of sales history is listed. It will show how many times the property sold and for how much. I suggest you ask the realtor for this info before you proceed. You will see if it transferred several times or if the seller is trying to make big buck on a flip deal.

Declining Market Values

If the home values in a certain area have declined between 10 to 15 percent year over year, then that area is considered a declining market. The geographic area can be a state, county, or town. The year over year is measured by comparing current prices to the same time last year. This information is obtained from the Board of Realtors data on sales and listing.

The appraiser will include this information in the appraisal and the lender will reference the data they have on site. If the house is in a declining market-value area, the lender has the right to take 5 percent off the top of the value and base the LTV on that, which means the mortgage will be less than you think.

Richard is buying a house in Bronx, New York, for $300,000 and applying for a $270,000 mortgage, which is 90 percent LTV. This county is listed as a declining market, and the lender is choosing to reduce the appraisal by 5 percent, making the value $285,000. This will reduce Richards's loan amount to $256,500, so he will have to come up with the difference. If he cannot, the deal will die.

To avoid falling into this situation, ask your realtor the following:

- The last two sales of the house, both date and price
- A list of recent sales in the area, similar to your house, also known as "comps"
- If this home is in a "declining market-value area"

Getting information like this helps in negotiating a price and will give you a comfort level with values.

Refinancing and the Appraisal

When purchasing a home, the loan amount is based on the contract price or the appraisal value, whichever is lower; when refinancing, it's based on the appraised value (because you already own it). The lender prefers to have an equity buffer, which is a gap between the loan amount and value. For you, this is savings in the form of equity. Remember, the more equity there is in the home, the less risk for the lender. Therefore, the amount of equity can affect your interest rate.

Property Inspections

Finally, it is time to kick the tires and find out if the home is in good condition.

A house is not a home if it is not livable, and a home inspection is the safest way to find out what is wrong, and I don't mean bringing your brother-in-law the plumber to look at the roof.

A professional home inspection is done either before or after you sign the contracts, depending on what the norm is in your area. If it's done before, it would be within a few days of when you put your offer in and before you sign the contracts. If it's after you sign the contracts, you should insert a clause that allows you a reasonable amount of time to have the inspection done and get out of the deal if the inspection results aren't satisfactory.

A home inspection is a visual examination of the house from the roof to the foundation and everything in between. The inspector will look at things such as the roof shingles, interior walls and ceiling, windows, plumbing and electric, heating and cooling systems, insulation, and other visible items. The inspector is looking for life left on items, defects, or sloppy repairs that could cost you in the near future.

There are many inspectors out there, either licensed engineers or trained inspectors. I prefer an engineer to do my inspections. An engineer is typically a retired engineer who needs or wants part-time work. These guys are licensed and experienced professionals. A licensed home inspector could be anyone who's had the crash course. The cost is the same for either and will range from $400 and up. I also suggest finding your own independent inspector, rather than taking one recommended by your realtor. Find an engineer in advance and ask him what the inspection will include, the fee, and how soon it can be done. Timeliness can be more important than cost because you only have a small window in which to do the inspection. You should ask how long the company has been doing inspections and how many houses they inspect a year. The realtor or homeowner will provide entry into the home, and you should be present. You will learn so much about the house by being there. Bring a camera to document things you want to remember.

If there is anything seriously wrong with the house, it will be fully documented in the report. You may want to negotiate the price if there are costly repairs that need to be made. Don't think that you'll be able to slash it to a bargain-basement price based on a leaky roof or a new boiler. The engineer will give you an estimate, and the sellers should allow time for you to get your own estimate for repairs. While the sellers may be willing to make the repairs, it's preferable to negotiate the price down rather than allow the seller to perform the repairs. You'll have more control and probably get a better job done.

Other "Scratch-and-Sniff" Tests

You should have the following inspections done, even if they are not required by law:

- Termite: Skip if your house is all brick, concrete, or glass.

- Radon: Checks for a carcinogenic gas, usually in the basement.

- Mold: Usually comes from water damage to the walls and ceilings (look for brown stains, new sheetrock, or fresh paint).

- Carbon monoxide: Odorless gas that makes you faint or sick, and can kill quickly.

- Lead paint: In case your kids or dog are going to lick the walls or snack on paint chips, which they sometimes do.

- Asbestos: A cancer-causing agent that may be in ceilings, walls, and insulation (look up at the ceiling).

- Septic: Waste can leak into the ground (gross).

- Water: Can you drink it? Bottled water is becoming politically incorrect!

- Oil tank: If it's buried in the back yard and it leaked, there will be big problems that you want the seller to pay for.

There are many inspections you can do on a home, depending on your personality type and budget. The lender no longer requires seeing these inspections, but you as the buyer will. At the very least, do a full engineer inspection to make sure the structure is sound!

Wrap It Up

- How much money do you have to put down? And if you need to come up with a greater down payment, can you get the money together?

- Are there any special features in the house that will affect the value, and who should be aware of them?

- Are you including anything in the purchase price other than the real estate?

- Are you covered in the contract with enough time to get a mortgage, and are you protected if the appraisal comes in too low?

- Is the home in a declining market-value area?

- Get an inspector lined up and find out which tests you will probably want to do, the fees, and how much notice the appraiser needs.

- Don't fall in love with the house until you know the deal is solid.

Chapter 5

What Mortgage Is Best for You?

When I began working in the Industry in the late '80s, there were just a few mortgage programs available to borrowers: a 30- or 15-year fixed-rate loan or a 1-year adjustable-rate loan. As we have seen over the past 10 years, more progressive, complicated, and riskier loan products have come about. The intention was to offer choices, which I am sure was a good idea at the time. However, greed got in the way and choice led to complication and then combustion. Now we are back to basics.

As I am very risk-averse and guide my clients down that same path, I always preferred the fixed-rate loan. Nevertheless, different strokes for different folks! Here, I will tell you about every possible loan product out there, whether it is currently available or not. Some of the products that are currently unavailable might return in the future.

I will begin this chapter with an overview of Private Mortgage Insurance (PMI) because it is an important topic for those borrowers who require it.

Private Mortgage Insurance (PMI)

The lender requires PMI if your loan-to-value (LTV) is greater than 80 percent of the home value or the purchase price, whichever is less.

LTV is simply a ratio representing the amount of financing you are requesting versus the value of the property (read more about LTV in Chapter 4). If you put 10 percent down, your LTV ratio would equal 90 percent. Therefore, if you do not put down at least 20 percent, you will have to pay PMI. The lender obtains the insurance on your behalf, but you will pay it monthly.

PMI insures the lender if the borrower defaults and there is not enough money from the foreclosure sale to pay off the loan. Do not think you can walk away from your home if the market plummets and your home is worth significantly less than your outstanding loan amount. PMI may not cover the entire loss, and the lender will come after you for the rest. Furthermore, a foreclosure will ruin your credit score.

Your PMI payment amount is affected by the following factors:

- Loan-to-value (the higher the LTV, the more the PMI will cost)
- Credit score (FICO—the higher it is, the best off you are)
- Purchase versus refinance (refis carry more risk if you take out equity)
- Owner-occupied versus second home (owner-occupied have less risk)
- Single-family versus two to four units (single-family homes carry less responsibility, thus less risk)
- Fixed-rate loans versus adjustable-rate loans (fixed rates pose less risk)
- Condo or co-op (condos have less risk)

The amount of PMI is calculated from a chart that all PMI companies and all the banks adhere to. Honestly, there will be a few dollars difference, but the range is close. You will receive an estimate for PMI costs prior to closing. That amount is added into your monthly housing expense when the lender qualifies you for the monthly payment.

The No PMI (Self-Insured) Loan

When a loan is advertised as *No PMI required*, it usually means it is self-insured. A self-insured loan has a higher interest rate to cover the cost of the mortgage insurance. With this type of loan, the lender pays the PMI premium out of the interest income made on the higher rate. When the LTV drops below 80 percent, the bank no longer has to pay the monthly PMI, drops the premium, and makes more net profit on your loan. Therefore, you are better off paying the PMI and saving the cost of the premium yourself when you become eligible. Why not save yourself the money?

PMI Is Tax-Deductible

PMI is now tax-deductible, where before it was not. So the idea of doing a self-insured loan so you can get the interest deduction is no longer applicable.

The following chart shows the difference in payment amounts for self-insured and PMI loans:

Self-Insured	PMI
Loan amount: $108,000	Loan amount: $108,000
Interest rate: 7%	Interest rate: 6%
Monthly payment: $718.53	Monthly payment: $647.51
	PMI: $56.00
Total: $718.53	**Total: $703.51**

Removing PMI

The rule is that once your LTV goes below 78 percent of the current home value, you can get the PMI removed. Consumer advocates tried to get it so it would automatically be removed by the lender, but lenders argued that it was too much work, and they would have no idea what the current value of the homes would be. Truthfully, the lender gets a piece of the PMI premium paid each month and hopes you forget you have it and continue paying it for the life of the loan.

So after years of struggle, they compromised. The lender now has to remind the borrower each year that she's paying PMI insurance, but it is the borrower's responsibly to get it removed.

The basic guidelines are as follows:

- An appraisal showing the current value must be provided and paid for by the borrower.
- The LTV must be under 78 percent.
- Each lender has their own guidelines, but at least 12 to 24 timely payments must have been made. Most lenders will require a minimum of 24 months regardless, but check with them if you think you qualify after 12 months.
- There cannot be *any* late payments.
- There can be no secondary loans bringing the combined LTV over 80 percent.

As the rules are not federal, each state is a little different in guidance. In addition, each lender has its own process to remove the PMI. Therefore, the borrower will have a bit of a runaround to find the right department to deal with. There will also be some fees and time involved, but it is worth the savings in the end. Sounds easy, but it is a real pain in the neck!

Fixed-Rate Mortgages

With a fixed-rate mortgage, your monthly payment (principle and interest) will be the same every month until you pay off the loan. The term of the loan may be amortized over 30, 25, 20, 15, or 10 years. As the chosen term to pay off the mortgage decreases, the interest rate offered also decreases. However, the monthly payment will be higher, because the mortgage is being paid off faster with bigger payments.

This is the most stable option because your interest rate is the same for the entire loan period, regardless of what the global economy is going through. If you do choose to make larger payments, or pay down a chunk of the principle, it will only reduce the total amount you owe and not your monthly payment. I suggest you notify the lender that you are paying additional money and you want it applied toward principle only. You can verify this by getting a payment history online or over the phone. Your total principle amount will be reduced, the total interest you pay over the life of the loan will be reduced, and the loan will be paid off in less time. *However, your monthly payment will be the same dollar amount.*

When you are deciding the length of your mortgage, remember that the lower the term, the higher the payment.

Years	Rate	Loan Amount	Monthly P&I	Total Interest Paid
30	6.000%	$100,000	$599.55	$115,838.45
25	6.000%	$100,000	$644.30	$ 93,290.89
20	5.750%	$100,000	$702.08	$ 68,500.81
15	5.250%	$100,000	$803.88	$ 44,697.82
10	4.750%	$100,000	$1,048.48	$ 25,817.19

40-Year Loan

A 40-year mortgage is the same as a 30-year mortgage, but your payments last 10 years longer, so your monthly payments are smaller. However, the lender will charge up to 1.5 percent of the loan amount for this privilege or increase the interest rate by approximately 1 percent for this loan, because you are holding its money longer.

While it may appear to have lower monthly payments, in the end the total amount you pay will be more than with a 30-year mortgage because of the higher interest rate and longer payoff. Don't do it!

Here is an example of the difference in monthly payment between a 30- and 40-year mortgage:

30-Year Mortgage	40-Year Mortgage
Loan amount: $100,000	Loan amount: $100,000
Monthly payment at 6%: $599	Monthly payment at 6%: $550
Total interest: $115,838.45	**Total interest: $164,107.57**

Adjustable-Rate Mortgages (ARMs)

With an adjustable-rate mortgage (ARM), the interest rate will change/adjust on the same date each year or period as indicated in the loan documents. The rate change is based on a chosen economic indicator (1-year T-Bill or 6-month LIBOR will adjust once a year or every six months depending on what you choose) plus a predetermined margin. There will be two caps (or limits): a term cap and a lifetime cap. The term cap places a limit on how high the lender can raise the rate each time it changes. The lifetime cap limits the maximum interest rate forever.

The choice to take an adjustable-rate over a fixed-rate mortgage should be made based on length of time the borrower will be keeping the property and difference in monthly payment. If a person knows that he will only be staying in a home for two years because he is being transferred, and the monthly savings is $200 a month, then it would be a good idea. However, if someone just assumes she will be moving in a few years or the savings is only $75 a month, then she might choose to get a fixed-rate loan. Remember, life gets in the way of your plans, so your short-term plan might get longer.

What Is Recasting?

As you pay down your principle, the interest payment is based on the lower amount owed. The monthly payment will include more principle than interest over time. This is called *recasting*.

If you have a loan where your monthly payment reflects this change, then your monthly payment will go down, or recast, with it.

Hybrid ARMs

A hybrid ARM is one in which the rate is fixed for a set period and then becomes an adjustable rate for the rest of the term. The monthly payment is still based on a 30- or 15-year term loan, with the most common initial lock periods of 10, 7, 5, 3, or 1 year(s), or 6 months. The longer the initial rate period, the higher the start rate will be. Therefore, a rate that is fixed for the first 10 years will be higher than a rate fixed for 3 years. You are reducing the risk of your payment increasing for a longer time, but the lender will have the risk that rates will go up and they will lose income because your rate stayed low.

In deciding between a hybrid ARM and a fixed mortgage, calculate the difference between the monthly payments for the hybrid ARM and the fixed-rate loan. If there is no significant difference in the dollar amount of the initial payments, then stick with the fixed rate. Always try to look to the long term rather than short, because you just never know what is going to happen.

A Few PITfalls with ARMs (Get It?)

The exact terms of the start rate, index (economic indicator), caps, and margins must be disclosed prior to the closing and then are all listed in the body of the Note. Make sure you read the disclosures when they come in the mail and bring them to the closing to compare with the loan documents. There are such things as errors in loan documents, and you want to make sure you are getting what you understood to be the terms.

Some ARMs have pre-payment penalties in case you pay it off early. This penalty can be a dollar amount or a percentage of the outstanding principle amount. Either way, it can be thousands of dollars and be a real bummer to pay, so try to avoid this. In some states, this is an illegal charge, but you would have to know this.

Make sure you are educated in the choices of economic indexes to choose from. As an example, an MTA will typically vary less than a LIBOR. (If you have no idea what I just said, perhaps you should research your economic indexes.)

Caps, Indexes, and Margins, Oh My!

Caps: Typical annual caps are 2 percent and lifetime caps are 6 percent. This means that your interest rate cannot go higher than 2 percent over your previous year's interest rate, and will never be more than 6 percent over the initial interest rate. If you have a loan product where the interest rate changes monthly or every six months, the chosen (time) caps should be no more than 1 percent, and there should be a lifetime cap of 5 percent. *Be wary of loans with only lifetime caps because your interest rate can reach the max immediately.* Make sure your cap is what they told you your cap would be! Bring all your loan disclosures to the closing!

Index: The index is an economic indicator chosen to dictate what the interest rate will be when it changes. It is the base number that changes each time your interest rate is due for a change. Common Indexes are 1-year T-Bill, Cost of Funds District (COSI), London Interbank Rate (LIBOR), and Monthly Treasury Average (MTA). You want to pick an Index that does not fluctuate terribly over the years. Historically, the MTA is the most stable index, but it is hard to figure out. If you really want one of these loans, then get some specific professional advice.

Margin: Your adjustment in interest rate is set by the index plus a margin. The margin is established at the beginning of the loan and never changes. An average margin on a residential loan is around 2.75 percent and will be the same for the entire loan. The margin is almost never negotiable for residential loans, but can be for commercial mortgages. The higher the margin, the more interest the lender can earn over the life of the loan. If there is a mortgage broker/banker involved, then the higher the margin, the higher the fee the lender will pay them for the loan.

Take a look at this example to see how your new interest rate will be figured:

Your loan is a 1-year ARM, with monthly payments based on a 30-year term.

Initial rate of 5 percent

Index is 1-year T-Bill (as quoted in *The Wall Street Journal*)

Loan margin is 2.75 percent

Caps are 2 percent annual and 6 percent lifetime

At the first anniversary of your interest rate change, the index for 1-year T-Bill is 6.17 percent. So the new rate based on the index plus the margin is this:

6.17 + 2.75 = 8.92 percent

However, the annual cap is 2 percent over the prior year's interest rate, so the rate will be less:

5 + 2 = 7 percent

Also, because there is a lifetime cap of 6 percent, the highest your interest rate can go over the life of the loan is this:

5 + 6 = 11 percent

Option ARMs

Like other ARMs, the interest rate for an option ARM is tied to an economic indicator (MTA, LIBOR, or COSI) plus a margin. What makes the option ARM different from other ARMs is your choice in payments. Each month, depending on your financial condition, you can choose a payment option that best fits your needs.

Typical options are *minimum payment due*, which is a very small amount set by the lender; *interest-only payment*, which is based on the actual interest rate; the *fully amortized principle and interest*, which is the real payment as if you had a normal fixed-rate loan; or *any amount* you want to pay without penalty. This type of loan is best for people whose income fluctuates due to commission or bonus payments. Qualification for the loan is based on the fully indexed rate plus principle.

This loan is also referred to as a negative amortization loan. If you only pay the least amount allowed, you do not even cover the minimum interest due. The unpaid portion of the interest is tacked on to the total loan amount, thus increasing your original loan amount. So instead of your loan getting smaller each month, it is getting bigger, thus negatively amortizing. Your interest is calculated on the bigger loan amount each month to boot.

This loan can be deadly! One big problem is that most people opt to make the minimum payments. (It is only human nature!) The borrower will promise the lender and himself that he will pay down the mortgage in chunks but might never do that for this, that, or another reason. It is very easy to say you'll pay more next month.

> ### *Funky Loans Are Not for Everyday People!*
>
> These loans are not for the poor or the financially irresponsible. Again, they were designed for people paid with bonuses or commissions who are responsible enough to make large payments.

Interest-Only Loans

With this mortgage, you have the option of paying just the interest for the first 10 or 15 years of the loan, although you can always pay any amount toward principle that you choose. However, if you never put a dime toward principle, then after that initial period, it will have to be paid back at an accelerated pace. If, for example, there is no principle paid for the first 10 years, the principle will have to be paid over the final 20 years, along with the interest, making the monthly payments huge.

Here is an example of how an interest-only payment might work out:

30-year fixed interest-only for the first 10 years

Interest rate 6%

Loan amount $250,000

Monthly payment for the first 10 years if you pay no principle: $1,250

Monthly payment including interest for the next 20 years: $1,791.08

This should be a feel-good loan because you actually see your monthly payment going down (by paying extra principle) rather than staying the same as it would with a regular loan. When principle payments are paid, monthly payments are "recast," or adjusted downward.

This type of loan was designed for people who earn most of their salary in bonuses or commissions and who will responsibly pay down chunks of the principle at a time. It is not for the person who can only afford to make the interest-only payment because he needs to eat. There is always a premium in fees or higher interest rates paid for this loan. So make sure, if you are going to take it, you are going to make those extra payments, or else it will be a feel-bad loan.

Pre-Payment Penalties

When clients ask me straight off if there is a pre-payment penalty, I know they were either burned before or read a book.

A pre-payment penalty can be in the scary fine print. Many of these ARMs have a pre-payment penalty if you pay off the loan in years one through three. The penalty can be upward of 3 percent of the outstanding principle, which can be a whopping amount to fork up. "Soft" pre-pay penalties are those in which you pay only if you refinance, but not if you sell the house; "hard" pre-payment penalties are those that you pay if you sell or refinance.

A partial pre-payment penalty states that you are allowed to pay off part of the outstanding principle each year without a pre-payment penalty. Normally, you will see that no more than 20 percent of the outstanding principle can be paid each year without a penalty. This seems like enough to me. If you do have a pre-payment penalty, please make sure you understand the exact terms as they are outlined in the actual mortgage documents.

Pre-payment penalties are a huge moneymaker for mortgage brokers/bankers and Wall Street. The longer the period, the more money the broker makes for selling the loan. The longer the period, the more the loan is worth to the secondary mortgage market. Don't be one of those people that you hear got conned; read the fine print and ask questions.

The Combo Loan

There are three main types of combo loans, each with its own distinct purpose.

80-10-10: This is a combination of two mortgages, which cannot be greater than 90 percent LTV, designed to eliminate the need for a PMI. The 80 percent (or slightly less) comes from your first mortgage (either fixed or adjustable), the second loan accounts for 10 percent (or slightly more), and then the balance is your down payment, which comes from your own funds. The second loan can be a fixed-rate second mortgage or a line of credit (HELOC). You can also use this method to lower the loan amount on your first mortgage from jumbo to conforming to reduce your interest rate.

80-15-5: This is the same concept as 80-10-10, except you only need to come up with 5 percent of the purchase price, as opposed to 10 percent. Although the interest rate and margin might be higher on the second mortgage due to the increased risk, you might still pay less than you would for PMI.

80-20: Again, this loan works the same as the 80-10-10, but the first and second mortgage combined equal 100 percent of the appraised value, which is basically a "no-money-down loan." This type of loan was available for a short period of time and luckily is nonexistent now.

The first mortgage can be any type of fixed or adjustable rate. The second mortgage can be a fixed-rate loan or a HELOC. You will need an outstanding FICO score, closing costs, and six months of housing payments in reserves. There is a premium of up to 1.5 percent charged on the first mortgage, and the interest rate on the second mortgage can be upward of 10 percent. However, you'll have to compare interest rates for the first and second mortgages to see if it's better to go this route or take one with PMI if you have cash to put down, keeping in mind PMI is now tax-deductible and might be the better choice in the long run.

Here is a sample comparison:

The Combo Loan

80-10-10 Loan	90% LTV with PMI
Purchase price/value: $200,000	Purchase price/value: $200,000
First mortgage LTV 80%: $160,000	First mortgage LTV 90%: $180,000
Second mortgage LTV 10%: $20,000	No second mortgage
Down payment 10%: $20,000	Down payment 10%: $20,000
First mortgage $160,000 at 6%: $959.28	First mortgage $180,000 at 6%: $1,079.19
Second mortgage $20,000 at 7%: $116.67	PMI monthly: $93.00
Total Monthly Payments: $1,075.95	Total Monthly Payments: $1,172.19

100 Percent Purchase Loans

This one loan covers 100 percent of the appraised value of the home. The loan may be a fixed or adjustable rate. The premium for PMI will be much higher due to the increased risk the lender is taking on. You must have a credit score over 680, assets to cover closing costs, and six months' worth of payments to qualify. There's a premium of up to 1.5 percent or higher added into the interest rate. This loan has been completely removed from society and if they bring them back after the dust settles, the lenders are more foolish than I thought.

The First-Time Homebuyer: Special Mortgages for Special People

Known under different names such as Community Homebuyer, My Community, and HomeChoice among others, the first-time home-buyer may get a break with loan requirements and sometimes interest rates. To help get folks into their first home, the loans are designed for borrowers who have limited savings, little or no credit profile, and nontraditional income sources. You can use gifts, grants, or loans to show your assets; utility bills and cancelled rent payments to create an alternative credit profile; and income from new employment, boarders, renters, Government Assistance, or public benefits.

The property type is one to four family houses, condos, and co-ops in limited areas. However, it must be the borrower's primary residence and not a second home or investment property. A down payment of 3 percent is allowed for a one or two unit, condo, and co-op; however, 5 percent down is required for a three to four unit.

To qualify, your gross income must be below 100 percent of the HUD (U.S. Department of Housing and Urban Development) median income level, or you must live in an eligible geographic area. This means that you have to make less money than the average person in your area does. You can find out from your lender the HUD median income level for your state or if the property is in an eligible geographic area.

For this loan you may also qualify with the income of a co-signor who does not live with you, referred to as a nonoccupying co-borrower.

The loan was originally intended to help people living with disabilities or the disabled and civil workers such as teachers, police, firefighters, and other workers. Today, it is for anyone who can meet the income requirements and qualify for the loan.

Fannie Mae Expanded Approval

This is one of those loans that your banker does not want you to know about. It is a mortgage product offered by Fannie Mae and Freddie Mac that saves the borrower tons of dough, but is a lesser moneymaker for all the loan guys. It is up to the individual lender to offer these products, and many choose not to due to risk or lower profit margins. The problem for the consumer is that if you do not know about the product or do not have an honest loan officer to tell you about it, you will never know it exists.

Even if you have less-than-perfect credit, lower income than you should, or very few assets, you may still qualify for a Fannie Mae loan. The interest rate may be slightly higher than a conventional loan, but it is *not* a sub-prime loan. You also may be eligible for a reduced interest rate after making 12 to 24 on-time payments, depending on the lender and its agreement with Fannie Mae.

Fannie Mae has loan levels I, II, and III, which reflect your ability to repay the loan. Levels are based on your credit score, amount of cash reserves, LTV, debt ratio, type of employment (self-employed versus traditional employment), property type other than a single-family detached home, secondary financing, and any foreclosure or bankruptcy. The higher the loan level, the higher your interest rate/cost.

Sub-Prime Mortgage

A sub-prime mortgage is a loan offered to people with any combination of blemished credit, undocumented income, and little or no assets. The definition came from "less than perfect" or below the primary mortgage guidelines: hence, sub-prime. The definition of a sub-prime mortgage is not what you read in the papers. They make it seem that every old lady, minority, or person who cannot read or write was offered a loan under fraud and duress.

The mortgages, designed for people who have a higher risk grade than average at any level of income or home price, brought credit to another group of credit-worthy borrowers. A sub-prime loan could be a $2,000,000 mortgage for a guy who makes $750,000 a year but has bad credit or can only put down 10 percent of the purchase price. It can be for a restaurant owner with a 770 FICO score who cannot document self-employed income. The sub-prime mortgage is for people who wanted or needed the mortgage but could not meet all the qualifications for a loan with "prime" guidelines and rates.

There were lenders out there, typically affiliated with large insurance companies, commodity companies, or Wall Street, that were willing to take the risk, but demanded a higher return on investment. This became big business and opened up to more groups wanting to get in on it, including the banks. As investor demand increased to buy these loans, lenders widened the product menu and guidelines to allow more people to obtain mortgages at the sub-prime level. The guidelines opened up, and then it seemed that anybody could get a loan (at a cost) and anybody could get into the game.

The sub-prime mortgage began as a good thing for marginal borrowers to obtain financing. It became a problem when it was offered to the completely unqualified borrower. An unqualified borrower is defined as a person who should not obtain financing at any level due to poor credit, insufficient income, or few assets. At the point of no return, many more people who were unqualified were able to obtain financing and buy homes. Real estate prices soared, mortgages grew larger, and the lenders created more products to offer people. The sub-prime products became more expensive and more complicated as investment vehicles, whereas the typical borrower could not understand (or did not care) about the actual terms of their mortgage. As anything, the steam was lost the house of cards collapsed. Unfortunately, the sub-prime mortgage began its humble beginnings with good intent but created a global financial disaster.

Stated, Low-, and No-Doc Loan

As part of the collapse of the mortgage industry, these loans are not readily available from most lenders. Following, I have explained each type of loan as they did exist and may once again in the future.

Self-employed or salaried borrowers sometimes cannot document enough income but can demonstrate an excellent credit profile with established work history. Examples would be the self-employed auto mechanic who cannot document his income but has been in business for 20 years, or the travel agent who has been working for the same company for five years but is paid as a consultant.

There are several different types of stated income loans with varying degrees of income and asset verification. The LTV will decrease with reduced documentation. The better your credit score, the lower your interest rate. Each lender will use its own nuances and risk levels to measure risk, so shop around. The loans go from least risky to riskiest, as follows.

Stated Income/Verified Assets

You must state your income in this loan, but the lender will not verify it. You can be salaried or self-employed; the lender will get verbal verification with your employer and/or a third party, such as a CPA letter, license, etc. Your stated income must correlate to your job description and geographic area. Lenders have industry charts for income and positions and utilize sites like www.monster.com and www.salary.com to verify income. You will have to provide documentation for your assets, which the lender will verify, and you will have to show 6 to 12 months' income in reserves. The minimum credit score ranges from 680 to 720 with this loan, and the maximum LTV is 95 percent.

Stated Income/Stated Assets

Again, you will have to state your income with this loan, but unlike the Stated Income/Verified Assets loan, your assets will not be verified. You can be salaried or self-employed. Proof of employment will be verbally verified with your employer and/or verified through a third party, such as a CPA letter, license, etc. With this mortgage, your FICO score must be over 700, and the LTV is capped at 70 to 90 percent, depending on the lender.

No Ratio

This type of loan is similar to the no-income-verification loan, but with this loan, the income section of the mortgage application is left blank. Therefore, there will not be any income-to-expense ratios utilized. Your employment is still verified. This can be a stated or verified asset loan, depending on the lender and the program. Of course, because the lender is taking a higher risk, you will have to pay a higher interest rate.

No-Documentation Loans and *True* No-Doc Loans

With this loan, you will not have to provide information on your employment, income, or assets, basically handing in a blank loan application. The loan is based on excellent credit and equity in the property. However, you'll have to pay a higher interest rate to compensate the lender for taking added risk.

With a *no-doc loan*, the lender might still verify your current-housing payment history to make sure you have experience in paying a housing expense and that the new monthly payment is not much higher than the old amount. They could ask for canceled rent checks or landlord statements, so be prepared.

With a *true* no-doc loan, they do not even verify your past housing history. You simply need to be alive and breathing at the time of the closing. The saying goes that the lender holds a mirror under your nose at the closing, and if it fogs up, you get the money.

FHA Mortgage

FHA mortgages are fixed- or adjustable-rate government-insured loans for owner-occupied homes. They are intended to assist in providing housing opportunities for low- to moderate-income families who might not otherwise qualify for a loan. The maximum LTV for these loans is 98.75 percent, and the minimum FICO score is 580 to 620, depending on the lender. Your down-payment money can be from a gift, and your employment history can be short term. Mortgage Insurance Premium (MIP), which is the PMI for this type of loan, is required for the life of the loan in most cases, whereas with PMI you can get it dropped once your equity reaches 20 percent. Programs cover single-family (one to four units) as well as multi-family properties (five or more units).

You cannot get an FHA loan directly through the FHA. They must be obtained through a HUD-sponsored lender. The FHA pays a lot of money to the loan originator, so they tend to attract a certain type. I do not particularly love these loans, so I refer borrowers directly to a large bank in order to obtain the lowest rate and fees. If you do go through a third party, make sure it is a reputable company that is certified by the FHA; this is called a mini-eagle. You want an experienced lender and never want to pay more than 1 percent in points, origination, or discount fees. This is why you want to go directly to a bank.

Mortgage Insurance Premium (MIP) is mandatory and expensive. The cost is 1.5 percent of the loan amounts' upfront fee and .5 percent paid monthly for the life of the loan. This means a lot of money.

Tip for Refinancing an FHA Loan

Note that if you refinance an FHA loan, you pay the MIP for the entire month, regardless of the payoff day. So try to close toward the end of the month, because you are paying for it anyway.

There is a new program that enables a borrower to cancel the MIP after five years. The loan must be for more than a 15-year amortization, the MIP must have been paid annually (not monthly) for a minimum of five years, and the LTV must be proven to be below 78 percent. The calculated LTV is based on original purchase price and value rather than current market value. If a loan is for 15 years, then this is automatic. A borrower may request the MIP be removed before the five years if the LTV has fallen below the 78 percent.

Veterans Administration Loans

This is a loan program similar to the FHA program, but it's available exclusively to veterans of the United States Armed Services and members of the veterans' families. The agency does not provide the funds for the mortgages directly, but partially guarantees the mortgages against potential default. Vets can put 0 percent down and avoid paying PMI with these loans, but they have high fees associated with them. You must live in the home you buy. Co-ops are not allowed.

Reverse Mortgage

A reverse mortgage is a loan that enables you to stay in your home if your savings runs dry by tapping into your home's equity to pay your living expenses. It is a "federally insured loan" that can be obtained directly from an authorized lender. It's best to go directly to a big bank to save on closing costs and get the lowest interest rate.

To qualify, you must be 62 or older, live in your home as your primary residence, and have equity available. The loan amount depends on the amount of equity you have available. You must own your home outright to qualify for one of these loans, and you cannot use the money from the loan to buy another home. You can disperse the money in one lump payment, monthly, or in a line of credit you use as needed. You do not have to pay interest back on the loan until the loan is paid in full; it must be paid in full when you or your heirs sell your home or you no longer occupy your home full time. Closing costs will be paid out of the original loan amount. You do not have to provide income or credit information to qualify for this type of loan. *Don't fall for the ads on late-night TV.* Go to a reputable bank for this loan, not a third party, to keep fees low. Make sure you discuss this loan with your financial advisor and go over the fees and payment choices in detail.

Free Information About Reverse Mortgages

Go to www.aarp.org to obtain a free booklet explaining the process. It is easy to read and is a great source of information before you even discuss reverse mortgages with a lender.

Home Equity Line of Credit (HELOC)

A HELOC can be a first or second loan that is secured with the equity in your home. It enables you to withdraw money as needed rather than get it all in one lump sum. The maximum line offered will depend on the value of your home and how qualified you are as a borrower. You can use and repay the line as needed over the term, which can be up to 30 years.

The interest rate is adjustable and typically based on the prime rate, although there are some products that offer a fixed rate. Ask about convertible rates, where you can fix the rate on the entire line or portion at any given time. You would do this when the rates go down and you want to fix it for a long period. There is a fee for this, but it's worth it.

You may get a HELOC to purchase a home, either as a first or second mortgage. When getting a HELOC for this purpose, make sure you fund the entire line at closing even if you do not need the money. You can pay it back within a week or two and use it when you need it. You do this in order to have the line considered "purchase money" and not a "cash out" loan. A HELOC is likened to a credit card if not used to buy a home. When you refinance your loan and add in your credit card debt, this is called a "cash-out" refi. The bank charges extra for a cash-out refi as well as limiting the LTV and the amount of cash out.

So you want them to think of the HELOC as purchase money, which has no effect. Provide your closing statement as proof to show you fully funded the loan when you bought the house. If you modify the HELOC in any way by increasing the line amount, fixing the interest rate, or reducing the terms, it will become a new loan and be considered cash out for purposes of refinancing.

I know this sounds silly, to take the money even if you do not need it. However, you do this in order to avoid extra charges to refinance the loan later on. It is just one of those crazy rules that you can get around if you know how.

Beware of "no closing costs," hidden charges, teaser interest rates, margin, lifetime interest-rate caps, and pre-payment penalties as well as minimum-required payment and annual fees when you shop around. The minimum-required payment can be $25, and your annual fee to maintain the account should be under $75. As with any home equity loan or line of credit, your home is used as security, so default can lead to foreclosure. Therefore, be sure to make your payments on time.

Construction Loans

A construction loan is needed when a house is being built and funded in stages. A builder sometimes sells a home from plans and then needs to get a loan to build it. The builder would have the buyer get her own construction loan to fund the project so the builder can save himself money and aggravation. The buyer should truly be compensated for bearing this exhaustive burden. Also, inquire if there is an issue with financial status and whether the builder cannot get a loan.

Qualifying for a construction loan is the same as with a regular loan, but many additional items are needed, including the plans, specs, building permits, and surveys. The contractor must provide resumés, insurance, and licenses. The loan amount is based on the value of the home when completed, but the money will be dispersed according to a schedule of work to be done. As work is completed, the value goes up and more money is dispersed.

Here are a few pointers:

- Go to a lender that specializes in construction loans and wants to do them.

- Get a "one-step" construction loan, where the construction portion will simply roll into a permanent mortgage when the house is complete. This will save tons of closing costs.

- Lock in the rate on the permanent mortgage at the time of closing the construction loan so you know what your rate will be. Also, find out what happens if the rates go down. Will you get a better rate?

- Find out what happens if you wind up not getting the permanent mortgage with that lender. Will there be a penalty?

- Save all receipts and canceled checks for money spent on soft costs and extra stuff you bought (like lighting) so you can be reimbursed for these. A lender will reimburse for money spent on the architect and engineers before the project even starts.

- Find out all fees before you proceed with the application. There can be many hidden fees such as multiple inspection fees every time more money is dispersed.

- Make sure the checks are not paid directly to the builder and are at least to you and the builder. This way, you know the builder cannot abscond with your money or use it for a different project.

- Find out the cost for a loan extension if the project runs long. They will always charge for this.

- If you own the land that the house will be built on, the lender will allow up to 75 percent of the value of the land to be taken out at closing. Because if you own the land the loan is treated as a refinance for a minimum of 12 months, the closing costs will be less, and the lender will give you extra money up front to work with.

- Construction loans are difficult and aggravating. Make sure your attorney, your lender, and your loan officer are experienced in them and understand exactly what you need.

Purchase-Rehab Loan

A "rehab" (rehabilitation) loan is necessary when you need to borrow money to purchase a home and then need additional funds to make improvements to it. This two-stage mortgage will cover the entire amount needed for the purchase and rehab. The first part of the loan, the purchase-money mortgage, is based on the original purchase price. The lender will typically fund 75 to 80 percent of the purchase price. The second part of the loan will act as a construction loan. As the work progresses, funds are disbursed from the rehab portion of the loan until the entire job is finished per the plans. After the house is completed, the two parts of the loan are rolled into one permanent loan, such as a 30-year fixed, based on the final, "as completed" value of the home.

Things you want to look for are a singular closing for both loans, a rate for the permanent loan that is set at the beginning of the process, and no pre-payment penalty in case you decide to take your permanent loan elsewhere.

Home Improvement Loan

If you already own a home, you can take out a home improvement loan in the form of a second mortgage. The second mortgage is treated as a construction loan, and the money will be disbursed as the work progresses. After the improvements have been completed, the loan becomes a HELOC or a fixed-rate second mortgage, which is set up similarly to a first mortgage. You will need to decide which loan is in your best interest for the long term.

With a home equity loan, you only use the money you need. With a second mortgage, you get a lump sum. The HELOC is best when you want to pay off the loan faster, want to have small interest-only payments in the beginning, or want to use the line of credit again. If you know that you need a fixed payment plan and won't pay off the loan quickly, the fixed-rate second mortgage is the way to go. The total loan amount is calculated based on an estimate of the property's value with the finished improvements ("as completed value").

If you have enough equity in the home before you do the work, it will be easier to take out a basic HELOC and then disperse the money as needed yourself. This way you do not have to provide any documentation for the work to be done or deal with a bank during the project. After the project is complete, you can refi the HELOC, based on the new value, and pull money out if you need to. This is much easier, and I would recommend this even if you have to borrow from a relative or 401(k), knowing you can get the money back after.

An Alternative to Bridge Loans

A bridge loan, also known as a "swing loan" or "gap financing," enables you to purchase or build a new home before you have sold your current home when equity is tied up in it. It's useful in a slow market when you might need time to sell your home. However, higher interest rates and fees may be associated with this loan.

These loans are expensive and hard to find. An alternative would be to take out a HELOC on your existing home and use it for the down payment on the new home. The key is appraising the house and taking out the HELOC prior to listing the house for sale. You cannot take out a loan on a house that is listed for sale, and it is a public record that the appraiser must report.

Wrap It Up

- Think about the kind of loan you need and want.

- Choose a fixed-rate loan if you are staying in the home for more than five years. If you are unsure, go for the fixed rate even if the current adjustable rates are much better.

- Are you able to put down 20 percent or will you need to deal with PMI or combined mortgages?

- Do you feel you qualify and can benefit from a government loan?

- Do you need to work on your credit score in order to qualify for a better mortgage?

- Are you buying a special property that requires additional mortgage approval?

Chapter 6

Where to Get the Best Mortgage

Fortunately and unfortunately, there are many places to apply for a mortgage today. The days of going to your corner savings and loan are long gone, and the abundance of choices has led to mass confusion.

Choosing where to go will depend on your personality type and financing needs. Finding the right source for your mortgage can be a combination of interviewing potential loan officers, deciding if they are a good fit for you, and ultimately feeling comfortable with the one you choose. Following, I will cover all possible choices from where you should not go, cannot go, and are able to go to for a mortgage. I will begin with where you should not go for a mortgage.

The Virtual Lender

The Internet is a fabulous tool for learning about terminology and using online calculators to figure out different loan payments; however, it is not the best place to get a mortgage. The virtual lender became big with the birth of www.Eloan.com, www.quickenloans.com, and www.lendingtree.com. These websites appear to be direct lenders, but in reality they are lead-generating companies.

The sites are designed to entice inquisitive borrowers to enter personal data in order to obtain a "free mortgage pre-qualification." This information is then sold to mortgage loan officers as live leads. The loan officers pay big bucks for this information, which is why they so aggressively pursue the potential borrower. Think of those amusing commercials with the folks going to sleep and jumping up to remember there are a bunch of loan officers sitting at their front door. It is not so funny when they are harassing you!

The bottom line is that there are only a few uses for the online mortgage companies. Use them for information, program definitions, and industry news, and even make use of their online calculators to play around with the payment schedules, but stop short of putting your personal data in. A free pre-qualification will cost you time and aggravation when the calls start coming in. Remember, nothing in this world is free!

The Geographically Undesirable Lender

Using a loan officer in Sacramento, California, to buy a condominium in Miami, Florida, might not be the best move. Using your cousin in Toledo to buy a co-op in Manhattan will be nothing less than foolish.

Although I say that the process of getting a mortgage is the same in all states, the method of closing them is different. Each state has different real property laws and mortgage closing procedures that make them all unique. I personally do not know how it works to close a mortgage in Montana, but I can get you a great rate. Your cousin in Toledo might have worked for a big bank the past 20 years, but he has no idea what a co-op is.

It is not necessary to go right around the corner for a loan, but do go to an institution that is familiar with your property type as well as closing procedures. It will make it worth your while to stay within range.

Do Not Go by Interest Rate Alone
When Comparing Lenders

To check and compare interest rates, go directly to the banks' listings. Many banks have a section on their websites called "today's rates." Try to avoid the rates posted in local papers or on the Internet. Interest rates change daily and the rates posted must be current to that day. Even so, your loan might have additional issues or features that will affect your rate. So do not believe everything you read or hear. Go to a reputable source.

When comparing interest rates, you must use the same loan, program, and day to get your quote.

For example: "I am buying a single-family home as my primary residence and need a $300,000 mortgage. I am putting down 20 percent, have excellent credit, and can verify enough income to qualify. What is your 30-year fixed rate, locked in for 60 days, and are you charging points for that rate?" You must compare apples to apples when shopping for an interest rate.

Where Can You *Not* Go to Get a Loan?

There are several agencies that the banks and government work with to sell, service, and insure residential mortgages. These agencies have a direct role in the mortgage process; however, they do not work directly with the borrower. The borrower gets their mortgage directly from a lender and the lender deals with the agency.

1. *Fannie Mae (FNMA):* Born out of the Great Depression in 1938, Fannie Mae was created by the Government to purchase mortgages in a consistent and uniform manner from mortgage lenders nationwide. It gave banks assurance that they could sell their mortgage portfolios, making them

comfortable in lending to homeowners. The agency became
so big and profitable that in 1968 it became a public company
and was no longer part of the government. The company
continued to purchase and service large pools of mortgages
until it grew into the monster that exploded in 2008. It has
been placed under government control once again with the
hopes of reform and stabilization in the near future. Although Fannie Mae advertises directly to the consumer, it is
for informational purposes only, not for lending.

2. *Federal Home Loan Mortgage Corp (Freddie Mac):* Created in
1970 to complement the work of Fannie Mae, Freddie was
also formed to buy mortgage pools from banks and secure
them to be sold on the global market. In some ways, Freddie
was more dangerous than Fannie Mae because of the more
sophisticated and riskier loans it bought. Here again, in 2008
the company went under government receivership and there
it sits almost worthless. Freddie buys mortgages in pools
directly from the lending institutions and the consumer may
not go directly to them.

3. *Federal Housing Administration (FHA):* Created in 1934 by
the National Housing Act, the FHA was created by the government to insure the payment of mortgages in case a borrower defaulted. After World War II, this Agency allowed
returning veterans to buy homes with as little as 10 percent
down at reasonable interest rates. This opened up the housing market and helped fuel a surge in homeownership and
the American dream. The FHA opened its doors to many
buyers who simply could not otherwise obtain financing
because of credit, income, or down payment constraints. To
this day, the FHA offers mortgages to many who would not
be able to obtain financing from conventional lenders. The
FHA has contracts with lenders to insure their loans; lenders
offer these mortgages directly to the consumer.

4. *Veterans Administration (VA):* Again, created to help returning veterans buy homes, the VA *guarantees* mortgages made by lenders to the vets or surviving spouses (until they remarry). The VA does not insure the mortgage, like the FHA, but guarantees to pay back a certain portion of the loan in case of default. That portion is determined by loan parameters, such as appraised value, purchase or refi, and property type. Although the loan does allow a higher loan amount as well as debt ratio, it can carry high closing costs for the borrower.

Where Are the Obvious Places to Get a Mortgage?

There are a handful of tried-and-true places to get a mortgage. While to many they seem common sense, there may be some surprises for you.

- Savings and loans
- Commercial banks
- Credit unions
- Mortgage bankers and brokers
- Your parents

Before choosing which one of these you want a mortgage from, you need to take a closer look at your needs and the different personalities of these lenders.

Commercial Bank vs. Savings and Loan

It is a personal choice between small or big, national or local, many product choices or personal service. A large commercial bank will offer competitive interest rates and many product choices. However, you will not go to your local branch for this loan; you will deal with a separate mortgage department sometimes clear across the country.

Some people do not mind calling an 800 number and speaking to a call center or being transferred from department to department.

A savings and loan is typically a smaller, regional bank. Again, they will offer great rates and a smaller menu of mortgage products, but you can go to a local office to do your loan application. By giving up product choice, you are gaining more personalized service while still getting a very competitive rate.

Credit Unions Are America!

Most credit unions are what savings and loans used to be—small community institutions that lend money to people to help improve their lives. However, not all credit unions offer mortgages or a full line of mortgage products. Those that do may lend their own assets and keep the loans or have a mortgage department that assists their members in finding and getting the best mortgage through affiliate programs.

What I like about credit unions that do offer mortgages is that their interest rates are typically lower than market, their costs and fees are often less, and their lending guidelines are more personal in that they are sometimes willing to bend the rules for members, a result of that personal touch.

However, there are drawbacks: mainly, the dollar amount and type of products they offer are limited. For instance, a credit union might not be able to offer loans over 80 percent loan-to-value (LTV) or loan amounts over a certain dollar amount. They also may not be able to do loans for second homes, investor homes, or other types of mortgages. Furthermore, they might only offer one product, say an obscure adjustable rate. If you fit into the box of what they do offer, you will usually find a great loan. If you do not belong to a credit union, I guarantee there is one that would suit you.

Mortgage Banker vs. Broker

Mortgage bankers and brokers are effectively the same, acting as a third-party mortgage provider. They work identically in that they go through the entire mortgage process with you, shop your loan and interest rate with lenders, and find the best one of the bunch. Whether you go to a mortgage banker or a broker, your loan will ultimately be with an institutional lender (bank or Wall Street).

Although they function the same way, the mortgage banker has the ability to use its own money to close your loan and then sell it to a bank a few days afterward. Therefore, the loan commitment letter, disclosures, and even closing documents can be in the name of the mortgage banker, and you might not know until the day of the closing which bank will hold your loan. In contrast, when you use a mortgage broker, you know from the start what bank you are borrowing from. However, it really doesn't matter because even if you get your loan directly from a bank, the bank will likely sell it.

You Mean My Mortgage Banker Is Not a Real Bank?

The issue I have with mortgage bankers is the use of advertising to lead people to believe they are a direct lender. I think even some of the very new loan officers who work at these places think they are working for a bank! I have heard things such as, "We do our own underwriting; therefore, we can make the decision to lend you money when other lenders might not" and "It is our money; therefore, we can give you a lower rate." *This is not necessarily true.*

Mortgage bankers always pre-sell loans before they close, run them through their warehouse lines (their own checkbooks), close the loans, and then send them to the real lender (bank or Wall Street) a few days later. The real lender will make sure the loan is complete, ready for its own mortgage portfolio, and then give the mortgage banker its money back. If more documentation is needed, the borrower must cooperate, even though the mortgage already has been issued. The rates are the same for a mortgage banker and broker because they are paid a premium from the bank to give them the mortgage.

Third-Party Lender vs. a Real Bank

In the past five years, more than 65 percent of all mortgages were obtained through mortgage bankers/brokers. Yes, your loan will ultimately wind up with a "real" bank, so why choose to go through the process with a third party?

If you apply for a mortgage directly with a bank, you are almost at their mercy as far as loan process, approval, and interest rates. If you go to a bank, then you have to go through the exercise to see if the loan will be approved. If not, you have to move on to the next one and start all over again. All the while, the clock is ticking for you to get a commitment letter over to the seller. In addition, if you are with a direct lender, you are stuck with their interest rate, even if the other lenders' rates are better. With a broker, you are not.

If you go to a third party and apply for your mortgage, the mortgage banker/broker will have the ability to shop your loan to different lenders. This way, you go to one party for your loan application, credit report order, appraisal, and all other documents required to process the loan. You should expect the third party to send out your application to three or so banks to make sure that you get the loan you want. If the mortgage brokers gets you three approvals and three commitment letters from three lenders, all three banks want the loan, so the final choice is made based on whoever has the lowest rate. The banker/broker does not care where the loan goes as long as you get a decent rate and the bank doesn't require excessive paperwork.

They also can act as your liaison with all parties involved. Rather than your dealing with a lender, the appraiser, attorneys, and a title company, not to mention the insurance company, your broker can do it for you. The bank could do that, too, but more than likely, at a bank you will be dealing with different departments. If you go to a broker, the loan officer can get more involved.

Furthermore, if there are some hard-to-deal-with issues, such as the appraisal coming in too low or rushing an approval, a broker can do that better than a bank because brokers have tighter relationships with the outside vendors.

One more thought on banks versus third-party lenders is based on the new rules for mortgages. If your loan is approved by a bank, you have the risk of the bank pulling the loan product from you, regardless of approval. If the loan was approved, committed, and rate-locked, the bank still has the right not to close. Recently, Washington Mutual went out of business and did not close any loans after they announced it. All those people who were ready to close had to scurry around and go elsewhere for a loan.

Though the phenomenon of banks going out of business overnight has become a pressing issue, there has not been legal precedent over what to do about a lost mortgage approval. Horror stories are surfacing about people being ready to close, but then the bank goes out of business or does not honor the loan approval. In this case, the people have already passed the timeframe to get a mortgage and presented the seller with a ready-to-close mortgage commitment. If they cannot get a replacement mortgage, then they cannot close and will lose the down payment.

Nothing in everyday contracts includes the language to protect the buyer if the deal goes dead because the bank goes out of business. So basically you are out of luck and you lose your down payment. Some buyers' attorneys are trying to add the language, but what seller will go for that? Make sure in this age that you have a backup plan with multiple approvals or cash in the bank.

Finding the Perfect Lender

It does not matter where you get your loan as long as you get the best service and the lowest rate. So how do you do this?

Ask around to family, friends, and colleagues for referrals. Your realtor will happily give you a few of their favorite loan officers to call. It is really best to get a few referrals and interview each of them.

There are few telltale signs:

- How fast do they call you back?
- Are they willing and able to answer your questions?
- How much information do they offer you in the initial conversation?
- Just because your cousin Eddie raves about his "guy," that doesn't mean he is right for you. You have to *click*. Think of the initial phone conversation as a first date. If you are not having a good time, why go out on a second date? There are as many loan officers out there as fish in the sea!

I have listed 10 questions to ask a potential loan officer. To give you an idea of an appropriate answer, I have provided what I would say. Don't take my answers as cut in stone, but use them as a guide for your interviewee.

1. How long have you been in this business?

   DS: I have been a full-time loan officer since 1998. (This is a *long* time! I believe that at minimum of 3 to 5 years is enough experience to know what you are doing.)

2. How long have you been with this company?

   DS: I own this company, so I have been here since 1998 and do not plan on going anywhere. (Again, this is rare. You want to make sure someone has been at the same company for at least one year. You also want to ask how many companies they have worked for. You do not want someone who jumps around, because if they leave, your loan might get lost in the shuffle.)

3. How do I reach you?

DS: You can call my office anytime; my secretary will patch you through if I am not here. I also have a Blackberry which is attached to me 24/7.

4. How do we do the application process? Can we do it by phone, fax, and e-mail, or do I have to come in?

    DS: I understand my clients are busy, so I usually complete the application over the telephone and then send the paperwork overnight or via e-mail if you prefer. Of course, you are welcome to make an appointment to come and see me if you wish.

5. How long does it usually take after you receive my paperwork to obtain a commitment letter?

    DS: Nowadays, it can take up to 30 to 45 days to obtain a full commitment letter. The days of the 48-hour turnaround are over. Also, the banks require a nearly complete loan application package from me before they begin processing the mortgage. So try and get me as much of your paperwork as possible early on.

6. How many different lenders will you send my loan to simultaneously?

    DS: I like to send most loans to at least three different lenders simultaneously. This way I ensure you will get a few loan approvals to choose from. Also, I can make sure that you will be able to take advantage of the best rates out there. We ultimately choose where we will close based on which bank gives you a commitment, but more so on which one has the lowest interest rate.

7. What is the process for us to lock in my loan rate?

    DS: Locking in is tricky and depends on when you are closing. I watch the rates like a hawk and try to judge when the best window of opportunity will be. I will probably call you when I think you should lock, but feel free to call me anytime. It does not cost you to lock in your loan, so we can lock in at one of our lenders and then move it to another choice if the rates go down and we still have time to close there. (I discuss locking in your rate in more detail in Chapter 8.)

8. These are the details of my transaction. How do you suggest we structure it?

DS: Based on a similar loan I closed last month, this is how I structured the deal. I will also give you one or two other ideas to look at. We will compare all of them as we work through the process, and you will decide which is best for you.

9. How many applications involving my loan type have you worked on and closed over the last year or so?

DS: I have worked on and closed 20 loans like yours last year. However, it really takes one or two to figure out how to structure a loan and which lender offers the best products for it.

10. Will I be dealing with you throughout the process or your staff?

DS: You will be dealing with both me and my assistant throughout the entire process. You might also receive calls from the underwriter or the closing department. Everybody here is familiar with your loan, so if someone is out, anybody can help you.

You will notice that not one question is about rates or closing costs. The initial interview with various loan officers should be about service and accessibility, not the loan. What you want to do is judge them on how quickly they call you back, how much information they readily give you, and whether or not the two of you click.

I always feel a bit attacked when a person asks me about rates and fees without even having a home or loan amount in mind. There are so many variables involved that it is impossible to pin down rates without having the purchase price, loan amount, property type, and closing date. I think loan officers who throw out a rate and a dollar amount for closing costs are just telling potential customers what they want to hear to reel them in.

Here again, I must stress the Internet might not be the best place to find a lender. When interviewing loan officers to gather information on service and how they would structure your loan, it needs to be more personal and direct. I believe this is the point where you will be creating a relationship with your loan officer.

So start by feeling the loan officer out in a conversation. If he answers your questions and, more important, asks you the right questions, then you will know if it is a good fit. Here are a few questions I ask potential clients in the initial conversation:

- Do you own a home or have you ever owned a home?
- What is your current housing expense and are you comfortable with that number?
- How long do you see yourself living in this house?
- How is your credit? Do you know your FICO score?
- Is your employment secure and income stable?
- Do you receive more than 50 percent of your income through a bonus or commission?
- Do you foresee anything in your future that might change your financial picture? In other words, will you be changing careers, expecting higher income, having large expenses such as college tuition coming up, getting a large sum of money from an inheritance, taking on additional personal responsibility (such as having your in-laws moving in with you), or other stuff like that?

If the loan officer was recommended and he does a good job on your loan, trust that he will also do right by you for the interest rate. It is also important for you to be aware of the market conditions as a good consumer.

Wrap It Up

- Begin by getting some names of loan offers regardless of where they work.

- Interview each one about herself and the type of institution she works for.

- Compare the pros and cons about working with each type of lender to see where your needs will best be met.

- Have your person all lined up and get a prequalification letter before you go shopping for a home.

- Have your paperwork together so you are ready to go.

- Never feel pressured into sticking with one person in case you change your mind and want to go in a different direction.

Chapter 7

The Loan Process

As I always say, finding the house is the easy part. Once you hit upon your dream home and negotiate the final deal, the real work begins. You will find yourself in a whirlwind of people and paperwork. Make sure you keep careful logs of phone conversations and a calendar of events. I suggest you keep a large folder of papers that you acquire over time and discard what you do not need after the closing. Please shred!

In the Mortgage Process, What Happens First?

It is best to do some preliminary research before you even go house hunting. First, you should seek out a lender and loan officer who will work best for you. Ask around to family, friends, and colleagues and get some names. Remember, even though Joe the loan guy worked out great for your best friend, he just might not click for you. See Chapter 6 for more information on choosing a lender.

I would begin thinking about lining up engineers, lawyers, insurance agents, and other professionals you will need for this transaction. It is good to have your people lined up so you do not have to stress over it after you find a home and make hasty decisions.

When speaking to your loan officer of choice, you will go over your particular mortgage needs and your financial situation as well as the property type and location, price range, and how long you plan to own the home. Be prepared to answer questions concerning your credit history, assets, and income.

If you are a first-time homebuyer, you will answer additional questions to determine how much you think you can afford for a monthly housing expense. More important is how much you want to pay for a monthly housing payment. For a new homeowner, my first questions are: What are you paying for rent and are you comfortable with that? Based on the information you provide, you will be offered several loan scenarios to think about.

I have listed many questions in Chapter 6 for you and the loan officer to go over during the pre-approval stage. It is at this time you will discuss what your current and future financial profiles will be.

Pre-Qualification

The first step in the loan process is the pre-qualification. Based on the information you provide, the lender will issue a "pre-qualification letter" stating the loan amount you are qualified to borrow based on current interest rates.

My letter is simply a boilerplate form with the date, your name and address, loan amount, etc., placed in. Based on information provided by you concerning your credit profile, income, and assets, you have been pre-qualified for a loan in the amount of X." Blah, blah, blah ... congrats!

You should get this letter before shopping for a home to demonstrate that you are a serious contender when putting in a bid on the property. It simply shows that you made an effort to find out how much you can pay and how much you can spend.

Because the pre-qualification is merely a show of action but not a real mortgage approval, there is not much value to it. You should update your pre-qualification every 60 days, as everyone knows it is not really worth the paper it has been written on.

The lender should never charge a fee for this service or run a credit report. If they insist on running your credit, move on and find someone else. (It is important to remember that this letter is *not* an approval for a loan. The formal application process has not yet begun.)

When you receive your pre-qualification letter, you will also receive a Document Checklist. It lists all the supporting documents you will need to provide for the actual loan application. A good idea is to start a separate folder for these documents and keep it updated throughout the process.

Credit Report

I hope you started with Chapter 1 of this book, but if not, this is a quick overview on credit and how it fits into the loan process.

Your lender obtains a tri-merge credit report from an authorized credit agency. A tri-merge is a combination of the three major credit bureau reports, showing your payment history and FICO score from each. The lender will use the middle (numerical) score as your rating for loan approval and rate pricing. The credit report is valid for 120 days; however, the lender might choose to run a new report right before the closing date to make sure nothing has changed.

Each time you go to a different lender to inquire about a loan, they will run your credit and you will have multiple inquiries. If you go to a mortgage broker or banker, they run your credit once and assign it over to the lender with your loan. Hence, you have only one inquiry, which will have less of an effect on your FICO score. This is not to say that the ultimate lender will not run your credit or rerun it right before the loan closes. So try not to do anything big, such as buy a new car, until after the closing.

Credit Check = Inquiry

Remember, do not let anybody run your credit until you are ready to do business with that person!

Application

The loan application is a package of several documents that need to be completed and signed (I have five). You want to work with a loan officer who completes the forms for you and just tells you where to sign. When clients say, "Just send it to me," I picture them pulling an all-nighter making sure that every item is correct and complete. If I do it, it takes 10 minutes of the borrower answering questions.

You can either complete them in person or over the phone; I prefer over the phone for speed. Once the application is complete, your loan officer will send the package to you, along with instructions and a list of other documents you will still need to send in. The required documents differ from borrower to borrower, based on the individual's employment situation and personal finances as well as the loan type. Documents can be sent back and forth by fax, e-mail, overnight express, or by snail mail.

Pre-Approval

In contrast to the pre-qualification, the pre-approval happens when you have actually completed and signed the loan application and provided the necessary documents for verification of your income, assets, and credit. At this point, the lender will run your credit report, and you will probably have to pay an application fee. In my opinion, anything over $300 is too much.

This document is really a commitment letter directly from the lender you have chosen. At this point, you do not need to have a property address. The pre-approval is good for up to 120 days. If you have not found a home by then, your lender can update this document for you.

They simply obtain your current pay stubs and bank statements and forward them to the lender. This is still not a full commitment letter until the property info is embedded in the approval. For this, you will need a house, signed contract, canceled down payment check, and an acceptable appraisal.

Pre-Approvals Are Mandatory in a Seller's Market

Note that realtors and sellers know the difference between a pre-qualification and a pre-approval. When the market is hot, hot, hot, they insist on the pre-approval; while in a soft market environment, they will take anybody with a pre-qualification in her hand, as long as she can breathe.

Technology and Your Loan

Over the years, technology has streamlined the mortgage process and sped up approval turnaround time. This is why you can get a commitment letter in two days. That is typically not necessary, but it is nice to know you can! Once your information is keyed into a mortgage processing system and your credit report and appraisal are uploaded into the electronic file, the information is transferred among lenders through cyberspace.

For instance, I enter all the info into my electronic processing system and have all of your supporting documents in my paper file. I can then take that electronic file and upload it to other lenders' sites for instant approval. The approval will come in 60 seconds (I kid you not) and it spits out a list of required documents and information. Simple things like pay stubs, W-2s, bank statements, and a canceled down payment check will typically be needed. More detailed items like extra information on the condominium building you are purchasing or how you receive money from a divorce settlement might also be needed. Everybody is different, so each loan file will also be a special package to put together. This is why it never gets boring for me!

I then take the virtual approval, all the documents requested on the list, and scan the entire package. I upload that scanned file into the lender's site again and, poof, it is there. The lender will then take the complete electronic file and a real person will look at it to make sure all the items are there. After it all looks right, I will get a commitment letter e-mailed to me. I then send it to you. This is all done without touching a sheet of paper and in the matter of a few days. This is not your grandmother's loan!

Commitment Letter

Once you're approved for the loan, you'll receive an actual commitment letter from the lender with a loan amount, expiration date, term, locked-in rate (if desired), and property address. Any outstanding conditions required by the underwriter are listed in the commitment letter, so please read the last page! Also, note the expiration date of the commitment and find out what you need to do if you need more time before you close. It could be as simple as updating a bank statement or a pay stub.

Send this letter to your attorney for review, and follow up with him in a day or so. Your loan officer and your attorney will go through the details with you. To avoid any nightmares, make sure you can meet every stipulation to get final approval to close the loan. If you miss the most minor of things, you could have big troubles at the bitter end.

Just because you have a commitment letter, do not think the lender is obligated to give you the money. Think about all the things that can change from the time of approval to the closing. You can lose your job, declare bankruptcy, blow all your money in Atlantic City, or the house you are buying can burn down. As the book is written after 2008, we know that the bank can change their guidelines rendering you no longer qualified for the loan program you were originally approved for. The bank can simply go out of business or stop offering mortgages altogether. As they say, it is not over until the fat lady sings.

Processing

Once your lender receives your loan package, your file is "opened" by a person in the lender office. The documents are placed in a specific stacking order, the data file will be entered into a mortgage-processing program, a credit report will be obtained, and all broker loan disclosures will be sent to you and other necessary parties. You will be contacted with any questions or if there are any missing documents, so make sure the loan officer has all of your contact info to enter in the loan file. The processing will continue as you collect the information needed. It is helpful to send as many documents as you can together the first time. This will expedite the process and help the office staff—whom you do not want to upset.

Many lenders will not allow a file to be processed until all the documents are in place, even the appraisal and sales contracts! In fact, many of my lenders now grade my mortgage files on completeness and time to close.

Banks Over-Disclose and Require Too Much Paperwork

New banking procedure requires the borrower to sign several disclosures pertaining to credit, loan type, and fees prior to the lender beginning the loan process. The file will sit there until the documents are signed and returned, so make sure to open all the mail from the lender. The problem is that the information can be inaccurate, but the lenders will require you to sign and return them regardless. This can be frustrating, but just know the fees and costs will be accurate and explained to you before the closing.

Appraisal

Again, there is another section on appraisal here, but I want to show how it fits into the process and approval. For more information on appraisals, see Chapter 4.

An appraisal determines the market value of real estate by comparing the property you want to purchase to three similar properties that have sold in the past six months within a 1-mile radius, preferably in the same neighborhood. Your loan amount is determined by the contract price or the home's appraised value, whichever is lower. Therefore, with a purchase, you want the appraised value to be at least the contract price. If you are refinancing your home, the value has to be a certain amount higher than the loan amount.

The lender or mortgage broker will order the appraisal on your behalf. An appraisal obtained by an authorized party such as a lender or broker may be transferred, assigned, and used by any lender your loan ultimately winds up with. If you go to separate banks yourself, they will each want to order their own. You might be able to get it transferred, but it will be a pain. If you already have an appraisal, the new lender will not use it unless it is less than four months old and they approve the appraiser. You are entitled, by law, to receive a copy of your appraisal. Ask for it. I send mine out as part of a post-closing thank-you package.

Engineer Report and Other Inspections

After you find a home, you should have various inspections done, including engineering, roof, termite, asbestos, mold, radon, water, and septic. The most important test is the engineering inspection, which examines structures such as the foundation, roof, exterior, windows, and heating and cooling systems—expensive things to fix.

Depending on the geographic area, you get the inspections done before you sign the contracts of sale, or you sign and then have a few days to get them. Either way, you need to get your inspections quickly. You should line up an inspector while shopping for a home so that you have one all ready to call. This way you can ask what the fee is, what is included, and how much notice he needs to schedule an appointment.

These tests are not necessary if you are buying a condominium or co-op, unless it is in a small building under eight units. With the small building, more things can go wrong, so I recommend getting an inspection as if it were your own home. In that case, you have a larger interest in ownership and it will be easier to get the engineer into the nooks and crannies of the building. With a large building, the unit owners do not have as much personal liability or responsibility, so I would not think an inspection is as important. Of course, feel free to get the inspections done on any apartment for the basics such as appliances, heating and air conditioning, and windows. You can find any engineer that is willing to inspect a condo or co-op in a large building, but the fee should be less than a house.

Building Information: Co-Ops and Condos

Although you could be the perfect borrower, the building you want to live in might not be as stable. You and your lender want to make sure you are not buying into a bad situation.

A condo/co-op is an apartment purchased in a building owned and/or managed by a company. The ownership of the apartment includes use and occupancy of the public areas. Occupants pay a monthly fee for maintenance and use. The fee covers all services provided, taxes, and other possible charges associated with the common ownership.

There will understandably be an additional layer of approval for a mortgage on a condominium or co-op. The lender will require information on the building and managing corporation, such as financial stability and occupancy. In a nutshell, the lender wants the last two years of building financials, Attorney General Filings, master insurance, and current budgets. The lender will also have a questionnaire that the building manager must complete. This is all normal procedure for us; for you it means more time and possible fees paid to the management company to do this work.

Obviously, you are not expected to have this stuff as a purchaser, but I would expect my realtor and attorney could get their hands on what is needed. If you are refinancing a mortgage, then you have been through this process before and should already have most of the paperwork the lender needs. Be aware: the management company will find a way to charge fees anyway.

Underwriting

The file is now ready to be reviewed on a higher level at the bank. This is done by an experienced underwriter who is trained to look for risk factors with the borrower or property that might affect the ability to pay back the loan. She looks for things such as gaps in employment, large deposits into a bank account without a documented source, or questions about how the appraised value was determined, among many others. The underwriter has the final determination of the loan approval. She will receive a complete loan file from the processor with all necessary documents pertaining to you and the property you are buying or refinancing. Typically, the underwriter will simply make sure that your file has all documents and you meet the criteria of the loan agreement. The underwriter may ask for additional information or have her own questions.

On occasion, a particular underwriter can kill a deal by virtue of her own set of rules. Some underwriters might request additional paperwork for a divorce agreement or more tax returns for a partner in a law firm, adding extra work for the loan officer and annoying the borrower. Sometimes the loan officer has to get exceptions, go over the underwriter's head, or simply beg to get the deal done. As the consumer, you will probably never speak to the underwriter directly, but just know your loan officer will get to her on your behalf!

Getting to the Closing Table

You are approaching the final leg of the tour—getting to the closing. There is still so much more to do that I have continued this adventure in the next chapter.

More Rules Mean More Paperwork

Under the new rules for mortgages, lenders are now requiring borrowers to review, agree, and sign off on the terms, interest rate, and fees prior to a closing. A disclosure must be signed and returned before a closing may be scheduled. These forms are arduous and confusing and were only created to cover the butt of the banks.

Wrap It Up

- Have your pre-qualification or pre-approval letter current and available when shopping for a home.

- Find your lawyer, insurance agent, and engineer ahead of time to avoid making hasty choices.

- Have all of your paperwork in order and ready to go when you need to begin the loan application to reduce additional stress.

- Make sure you open all correspondence from the lender and respond to all requests promptly as not to delay the process.

- Understand the terms of the loan and make sure you are privy to any changes in appraised values, loan amounts, and interest rates.

- If you are buying in a co-op or condo, make sure the bank is receiving the additional documentation needed from the attorney, realtor, and building managers.

- Make sure you get your commitment letter within the time required in the contracts. If there are issues that will delay it, give your attorney enough notice to tell the seller and ask for more time.

- Get ready to close!

Chapter 8

Interest Rates, Closing Costs, and the Closing

This is the stressful part because lenders usually wait until the last minute to do final reviews and request crazy things at the eleventh hour. All parties will work together to smooth out the organized chaos, and you will close on the property. Although the whole process can be traumatic, once you close you will forget all about it!

This is when you will be doing the last-minute running around, getting papers that the lender should have asked for weeks before, making sure your insurance is in order, transferring money for the closing, and waiting for the exact date and time of the closing to be worked out.

Contact your lender and make sure you do not need any other paperwork and that your rate is locked through the closing date. You also want to verify the bank fees due at the closing.

Make Sure You Have a Lawyer—a Good Lawyer

First thing first: if you are buying a home in a state where real estate brokers prepare the contracts, have an attorney review it. Realtors are not lawyers, and they are not always representing your interests.

Many states do not require using an attorney in a real estate transaction. I am based in New York and am an attorney. I cannot imagine why anyone believes that a realtor can do the same job as an attorney. Would you let your dentist perform open-heart surgery on you or have your vet pull your tooth? You are spending so much on the house; spend a little more and get a lawyer.

In some cases, the attorney who represents the lender will give you a discount to also represent you as the buyer. This happens in many states where the buyer's attorney also represents the lender and/ or the title company. In New Jersey, the buyer's attorney is also the bank's attorney. In Connecticut, the buyer's attorney is also the title company's and the bank's attorney. In Florida, you use an escrow company, which is the title company but also represents the lender. I never have a problem with this as long as it's disclosed right from the start and you're receiving some discount in fees, say 25 percent.

When Is Your Rate Your Rate?

The interest rate quoted to you might not actually be the one you wind up with until it is "locked in."

Locking in your interest rate means that your rate is guaranteed for a period of time, preferably until the closing. Do not assume the rate quoted initially is a done deal. An interest rate can be locked in at time of application, anytime during the loan process, or right before the closing. It is imperative to know when it is locked, how long it is good for, and whether there will be a charge.

A rate quote is simply a quote when loan shopping. It is the current rate if you were to close at that moment in time. Many loan officers will quote an extremely low rate just to get you in the door. If it sounds too good to be true, it probably is. When shopping, make sure you ask for a quote on a rate locked for at least 30 to 60 days. If one guy is much lower than the rest, be careful.

When you begin the application, ask the loan officer what interest rate she is using to qualify you and find out if that will be the interest rate. It probably will not be unless you are clearly locking it in. At this point, I would ask her to explain the process and method for locking in the rate.

You can lock in your interest rate at any time during the approval process. You will have a better idea of when you will be closing and will therefore know how long you need to lock in for. At this point, you want to have much communication with the loan officer as to her rates.

Your rate really becomes your rate once you lock it, so know it.

Your Interest Rate = Base Rate + Add-Ons

The new thing now is for banks to advertise what is known as the "base rate." From there, they add things on for every nuance in your loan, such as number of units, property type, ownership, FICO score, loan-to-value (LTV), lock period, etc. When getting rate quotes, make sure you tell the loan officer the entire story and ask them what the add-ons will be.

The Lock Game

Your interest rate is floating until it is locked in. Once locked, you will close with that rate.

Interest rates are extremely volatile and can fluctuate several times a day. Trying to lock in at the lowest rate becomes a game and even a gamble. People who try to win usually lose. What I suggest is that you pick a rate that you would be happy with and strive to get it and lock it in. Once it "hits," do not gamble and wait to see if they go down. If you try to save ⅛, it might cost you ¼ point. Just know you will never find the lowest rate out there and will never lock it in at the bottom. If you knew how to do that, you'd be running the Fed!

The Lock Process

It is important to understand the process of locking in your rate with your lender, broker, or loan officer. The process is different depending on where you are getting your loan. It is also quite different if you are getting your mortgage directly from a bank or through a mortgage broker/bank.

Do we lock in the rate verbally or in writing? Most places lock in interest rates over the phone. Some lenders do require you to sign a written confirmation, and I suggest you at least get one as proof.

How long should I lock my rate in for? It is best to have some idea of when you are closing before you lock in a rate. Banks will lock in your rate for 15, 21, 30, 45, 60, or 90 days. The longer you lock the interest rate in for, the higher it will be or the more it will cost you.

If you are locking in your rate for 90 days, it means you think the rates are going to go up. If you think this, perhaps the bank agrees and they want to hedge their bets. You hedge your bet by locking in for a longer period of time, and so the bank hedges by charging you more, just in case the rates go up and it winds up costing them more.

Locking In Your Rate

15 days	21 days	30 days	45 days	60 days	90 days
6.000%	6.125%	6.375%	6.625%	6.750%	7.000%

Or pay additional points:

0.000%	0.250%	0.375%	0.625%	1.000%	2.000%

What if I need to extend the rate lock? When you lock your rate, you assume you will be able to close within that time. However, things come up that require more time and you might need a few more days to close. If your rate lock expires, you should not lose it, but you will need to extend it. Again, different lenders have different policies and fees, so ask when you lock in what you need to do.

Some banks will charge a flat fee to extend your rate for a few days or even a week. Some lenders will charge a percentage of the loan amount to extend the rate. An idea would be ⅛ point for three days, ¼ point for a week, ½ point for two weeks, and so on. Some banks will say you can extend the rate but your actual rate will be the worse option between the current rate and your original locked-in rate. Lastly, some banks will charge you .003 points per day no matter how many days. They are all different, so understand how your lender will work it out. Make sure you lock in for more than enough days and find out if you can get a second extension if you need it.

What if the rates go down after I lock? Most people get awfully mad if they lock in the rate and then they could have gotten better. A missed opportunity no matter how small can depress most borrowers. If you cannot deal with it, then ask the loan officer about the float-down feature.

Most lenders will say they have a float-down, but they are not too favorable for the borrower. Why would they want to give you the lower rate and lose money? You really need to understand the parameters, such as how much lower the rates have to get, if you will get the exact new lower rate, if you have to pay for it, and how many times you can get a float-down.

As an example, a lender will allow you to float your rate down, but the rate has to be at least 1 percent lower and they will only lower your rate by half. In addition, they will only let you do this once.

On occasion, you can threaten the loan officer that if he does not lower your rate, you are going elsewhere. I would do my research, have evidence of a competitive rate available, and be ready to walk. I had a friend who went to a bank for her loan and locked in. After she locked in there, the rates went down three times. Each time I sent her a current rate sheet, which she forwarded to the loan officer, and each time he lowered it without charge. I felt he was a sucker and was desperate to keep the loan, but you never know!

What is the difference between locking with a bank versus with a mortgage broker? There is a huge difference here, which is one of my biggest reasons to use a third party to obtain a mortgage. If you go directly to a bank, not only are you at their mercy with loan approvals and timeframe, but you are stuck with their interest rate even if their rate turns out to be the worst one out there. You can threaten to go elsewhere, but remember, you must have the time to start over again.

If you go to a mortgage broker/banker, they have the ability to send your loan to a few lenders simultaneously for approval and thus can shop your rate around. For me, acting as a mortgage broker, this is how it goes: I process your loan and send it to three different lenders for approval. Assuming all three banks can do it, I work the loans until they are ready to close at each of them. All along, we are watching the interest rates and comparing them. Let's say you are closing in 90 days and are getting nervous that the rates may go up. I lock you in at Bank A for 60 days at a decent rate. This way, you know you have a rate and can sleep easy. We keep watching them, and now 30 days before the closing the rates go down and I lock you at Bank B at an even lower rate. Two weeks before the closing, the rates pop down and, boom, I lock you in at Bank C and have two weeks to gear it up to close.

Remember, it does not cost the borrower to lock in an interest rate, so there is no cost or penalty to you for not going to the banks that also approved your loan and locked in the rate. The mortgage broker will disappoint the lender and might have a problem with them if they do this too often. However, it is not your burden; that is why you hired a mortgage broker. This is my only foolproof way of getting a client the lowest rate. It is a lot of work, but worth it at the end. So if you are using a mortgage broker, ask him what his method is and hope he reads this book!

What Really Affects Mortgage Rates?

In a nutshell, short-term rates are adjustable rates and are reflective of the short-term bond rates and movement. Long-term rates (30-year mortgages) are affected by the secondary mortgage market; that is, how much your mortgage can be sold for later on.

There are several factors affecting mortgage rates, including inflation, unemployment, the price of oil, the value of the U.S. Dollar, and the bond market.

While short-term interest rates can adjust for inflation and retract in slowing economies, long-term rates (30-year mortgages) increase during periods of inflation because the banks want to protect themselves in the future.

The unemployment rate affects short-term mortgage rates because the Fed adjusts short-term rates to ignite the economy. If unemployment rates are high, the Fed may lower interest rates so consumers have more money to spend, thereby boosting the economy. If, on the other hand, unemployment rates are low, the Fed may raise interest rates to slow inflation. Short-term interest rate adjustments affect adjustable-rate mortgages (ARMs), because banks adjust their interest rates based on how the Fed reacts.

The cost of oil affects interest rates in a couple of ways. First, with high oil prices, consumers are spending more money at the gas pump and heating their homes so they have less money to spend in the economy, including the housing market.

The value of the U.S. Dollar also affects interest rates. If the dollar is weak, bond prices decrease because foreign investment drops. This, in turn, hikes up the yield on government bonds to encourage foreign investment. Yields directly correspond with interest rates. Therefore, if the yield increases, so do interest rates on long-term mortgages.

The bond market has a direct effect on long-term interest rates. Banks rely on foreign investors to invest in U.S. Treasury Bonds and generate enough revenue to offer low interest rates on long-term mortgages. With a slowing economy in the United States, these investors become warier of investing in U.S. bonds, causing an increase in the yield on government bonds, resulting in increased mortgage interest rates. Of course, the opposite takes place during a heated economy.

Many people expect long-term mortgage rates to drop when the Fed drops the prime rate; however, the prime rate only affects short-term rates such as those for consumer lending, home equity loans, credit cards, auto loans, and student loans. It has no effect on long-term mortgage rates. For the banks, it's all about the market and making a spread: how much can they lend out, and at what profit margin.

The Secondary Mortgage Market

The most important factor that affects our American mortgage rates is something called the secondary market. Banks pool their mortgages and sell them to Fannie Mae or larger Wall Street Institutions in bulk. When they sell the mortgage portfolio, they get the entire amount back plus a premium. The institution that bought the pool cuts it up and sells it in pieces to other investors such as foreign governments, international banks, hedge funds, and other U.S. institutions. From there, they might cut it up again. So your mortgage is no longer Mr. Smith's loan; it is a piece of a global investment constantly being pooled and sold all over the world. Your house is no longer the American Dream, but just a global investment vehicle.

When the secondary mortgage market collapsed in 2008, there was a complete freeze on lending at every level. If the global investors will not buy pools of loans then the local banks that make mortgages cannot get the money. This system has a domino effect that unfortunately works from top to bottom and up again.

Closing Costs

I will not go through the particulars of closing costs, because they are different with each deal, state, and lender; but they are all basically the same.

The lender is required to give you a good-faith estimate of the costs associated with closing on the property within three business days of receiving your application for the loan. Keep in mind it's merely an estimate, and the final costs could and probably will change. While it's only an estimate, you can use it to compare costs with quotes from other lending institutions.

The different categories of closing costs include bank fees, advance fees, reserves, title charges, government charges, and any additional charges. Typical closing costs will range between 3 and 6 percent of the mortgage amount (not the contract price). A three-point spread is significant but is mostly due to the value of your home or your mortgage loan amount and the rates for various costs in the state where the property is located.

The Lure of "The No Closing Cost" Mortgages

No-cost mortgages are nothing more than a great form of advertising. I advise reading the fine print. If all goes well, you might save a few hundred bucks, as the lender may waive the application fee and/or the appraisal fee. More than likely, they are not waiving all the title fees and government recording fees, so what are you saving? Be aware that your closing costs might be hidden in an increased interest rate, and make sure there is no prepayment penalty.

Origination Fees, Discount Fees, and Broker Fees

Points, origination fees, discount fees, and broker fees are paid as part of your closing costs. No matter what you call it, a point is a point: 1 percent of the loan amount. To put that into plain terms, on a $100,000 dollar loan, one point equals $1,000.

Origination fees are costs associated with processing your loan. A lender will say it is a fee to "originate," or obtain, your loan.

Broker fees are costs you pay to your mortgage broker, the liaison between you and the lender. Your mortgage banker or broker is paid by the bank, so she should not be charging you a broker fee in addition.

The higher the interest rate on your loan, the more your broker/banker will be paid by the bank. If she offers you a lower interest rate, she will make less money from the bank but will charge you a fee for the reduced rate. This is referred to being paid on the back end (from the bank) and the front end (borrower); the total will equal what the lender wants to make.

Discount points are additional costs that you pay the lender in order to secure a lower interest rate. The sales pitch is "pay a point and you can lower your monthly payment"; I call that pre-paid interest in which the bank is ensuring themselves more income on your loan. If you use a mortgage broker/banker, I can guarantee you that he is making a little more money off your loan.

Do the math:

Loan amount: $100,000

Rate: 6.250%

Monthly payment: $615

Pay 1 point ($1,000) to reduce rate to 6% = monthly payment $599

Monthly savings in mortgage payment: 615 – 599 = $16

How many months of savings does it take to get back the point?

$1,000 ÷ $16 = 62.5 months

Not worth it!

The Annual Percentage Rate (APR)

This takes into account your interest rate and one-time fees associated with the loan. These one-time fees generally consist of discount points, credit report fees, and mortgage insurance. The one-time fees are spread over the life of the loan, and the annual percentage rate (APR) becomes your interest rate in effect. The larger the difference is between your interest rate and APR, the more the closing will cost. The APR is standardized across lenders, making it easier for you to compare one lender to another.

Find this confusing? Just remember, the interest rate and APR should be very close, perhaps ¼ percent difference. The bigger the difference, the more points you are paying.

Waiving Escrows

The banks want you to escrow for your real estate taxes and insurance and have the bank pay them for you. This way they are insured that they are paid on time. What you do is tack on ¹⁄₁₂ of the annual taxes and insurance amount to each mortgage payment. So, if your real estate taxes are $11,000 for the year and insurance is $1,000, you will pay an extra $1,000 a month to the bank with your principle and interest payment. The bank collects the money, keeps it in a special escrow account, and pays them out when they are due.

Principle, Interest, Taxes, and Insurance

Known as PITI, it is the lingo used by lenders for your monthly payment of principle, interest, taxes, and insurance. When qualifying you for the loan, they throw this term around a lot.

The bank will pay you a small percentage of interest for the money in the escrow account (1 to 2 percent), but they will make an enormous return on all the escrow money they hold and invest.

You will have the choice of escrowing or not escrowing. However, in some states the bank is allowed to charge you a fee (¼ percent point) to waive the escrows. In some states, it is against the law, and they cannot charge the extra fee, but the rate might be a little higher in that state to compensate them. Some lenders will force first-time homebuyers to escrow because they fear this is new to them and they might screw up. Banks might also make borrowers escrow if they are putting down less than 20 percent of the purchase price. Again, these are bank-by-bank, state-by-state rules.

It is a personal choice, and most people like the thought-free, hassle-free method of escrowing. Others prefer to have the money in their own account until it is due.

Junk Fees

Junk fees are fees you are required to pay and that seem to crop up out of everywhere. Pretty much everybody has their hand out at the closing; just make sure you don't get squeezed. Your lender should document many of these fees in their good-faith estimate, but not all of the fees by all the parties are required to be included. They're generally non-negotiable but, in any event, the time to negotiate them is before signing the loan, not at closing.

The following is a list of some of the junk fees I would call acceptable:

- Application fee.
- Processing fee.
- Underwriting fee.
- Document preparation fee.
- Credit report fee.
- Appraisal fee.

- Appraisal review fee.
- Fannie Mae certificate.
- Flood certificate.
- Overnight fees.
- Lender's attorney fee.
- Attorney travel, if he has to drive more than 50 miles.
- Attorney overnight fees. (I would fight the copying fee and document review fee: she is already getting paid, and copying the file is part of the job description.)
- Title charges. These are a mixed bag of the premium and a mixed bag of miscellaneous fees. Have your attorney go through each item with you at the closing. There are small, unnecessary fees that will slide through unless you make a fuss.

Mortgage Life Insurance Is a Crock

Mortgage life insurance is a type of insurance policy your lender sells that provides for full repayment of your mortgage in the event of your death or that of your spouse. Although this may sound enticing, do not let your lender trick you into purchasing such a policy. Regular-term life insurance will provide you better and more affordable coverage. Term life insurance is less expensive than mortgage life insurance, and it moves from house to house if you move. Mortgage life insurance requires you to be in the same house and to have made payments for a certain number of years (normally a minimum of 10 years) to be able to collect. If you refinance, the time period begins anew, making it even more difficult to ever recover. Term life insurance will have a shorter payment period and will enable your family to recuperate even more money than is remaining on the mortgage.

Homeowner's Insurance

This is insurance in case the house burns down. The lender will require *full replacement value* coverage. This means the insurance company will pay the amount it will cost to replace the house to its original condition, even if it costs more down the road. As a homeowner, you want to know that your insurance company will pay the amount of money needed to build the home for *today's* costs, not for when you bought the house. Make sure you have replacement value and that the terms are outlined in the policy. For a purchase, they will require proof of payment for 12 months and a paid receipt; for a refinance, only 6 months is required.

Day of the Purchase Closing

You will do a final walk through the house to make sure the place is left empty, is broom clean, nothing is broken, and that everything still works. Flush toilets, run the water, start the appliances, and check the air conditioners and thermostats. If there is a pool, check that, too. Here's a good one: make sure all the ceiling lighting fixtures, the light-switch covers, and window screens and storms are there.

You Cannot Go Swimming in the Winter

If you buy the house in the winter, how do you check the pool and the air conditioner? You can't, so see if you can escrow or hold a few hundred dollars until the spring.

At this time, you will have arranged with the utility companies and all services to have the accounts stop with the sellers and switched over to your name with a new account. This way you are not left with any balances to pay.

Your attorney will have the final figures for the closing the day before. Go over them and then run to the bank to pick up your certified checks. If you have a dispute, it is best to work it out before the closing, but bring all of your loan paperwork and paid receipts with you just in case.

Remember to bring photo identification and all mortgage documents to the closing.

Closing for a Purchase

Once the lender is ready to close, they will begin coordinating the closing date and time with you and all parties involved. Depending on which state you are in, there can be as little as one other person in the room or as many as 10. In New York State, I can count at least four suits in the room! Your lawyer, seller's lawyer, bank attorney, title company rep, realtors … oh, and you!

Once the closing is set, the lender will prepare the documents needed for signature, order the money to be transferred, and do any last-minute checks on credit employment or assets. You might be reminded to bring a few things to the closing such as proof you sold another home or your latest pay stub.

Your attorney will tell you how much money in certified funds you will need to bring to the closing, typically the day before closing. Do not forget to bring a government-issued, active photo ID to the closing (e.g., driver's license or passport) or you will not be able to sign the required paperwork.

Typically, purchase closings are scheduled for the afternoon to ensure the funds needed are transferred in time. Therefore, you will have the morning to do a few things. Buying a home is a big deal, so take the whole day off work, and the following day if you can. Although this whole process can be stressful, once you close, you will forget all about it! Did I say that before?

Closing for Refinances

The closing is more flexible with a refinance because there are usually no time constraints and fewer people involved. Even if the bank is ready to close, you can wait until you are ready or locked in at the lowest rate available.

Depending on the state, the lender will have an attorney, title company, or escrow agent represent them at the closing and arrange for the money to be dispersed. You are not required to have an attorney represent you at a refi closing. I don't think it is necessary, but you can have one if it makes you feel better.

Your final closing costs are itemized and taken directly from the mortgage proceeds at the closing. Unless you are paying off a mortgage and other bills that total more than the new mortgage, there is no need to bring a check to the closing. Do not forget to bring along your government-issued active photo ID such as a driver's license or passport.

With a refinance, there is a three-day right-of-rescission after the closing takes place. This means you have three business days (Saturday included) to review the documents and make sure the loan is right for you. After this waiting period, you give the closing attorney permission to release the documents and all monies.

Post-Closing

After the closing, you will receive a post-closing package from your lender with a copy of your appraisal and other important documents. Your attorney will also give you a package with copies of all the documents signed at closing. Keep these documents in a safe place, and give a copy of your closing statement to your accountant for tax purposes.

Also, make sure that you receive a copy of your recorded deed and mortgage. This can take up to six months, depending on the county the property is in. Make a note on your calendar for six months after the closing to follow up on recorded documents. Your attorney might get them for you. Either way, you want recorded deed and mortgage in a safe place for when you sell your home.

A Note from My Mother ...

After you buy a house, you should always get the locks changed. You have no idea how many spare keys are floating around. Do you really want to get an early-morning visit from the seller's distant cousin?

Call a locksmith, and at the very least get the lock cylinders changed. If you are having work done before you move in, hand out keys freely, knowing you are getting the locks changed after they all leave.

Wrap It Up

- Get yourself a good lawyer lined up before you even find a house. After your offer is accepted by the sellers, the first thing the realtor wants to know is who your attorney is, and you do not want to go scrounging around at the last minute.

- When shopping for a loan, ask for a good-faith estimate and compare fees. Remember, everyone should be around the same range in cost; if one is much lower, there is something wrong.

- Try to avoid paying points, but know the value in it sometimes. Do the math to get it right.

- Do not be so concerned about the APR and the exact fees, but do understand the process of setting the rate and locking it in.

- Know what the terms are to extend the rate or float it down if need be.

- Go over your closing costs the day before the closing so you are not crazed the day of and miss something.

- Bring an active, government-issued photo ID to the closing, make sure your checks are certified, and make sure you have money in the bank to cover additional fees.

- Call the locksmith.

Chapter 9

Types of Property

My brother would love to live in a tent, but he cannot get a mortgage for it. I once stayed in a tree house on vacation, but could not get a home equity loan on it. There are many different types of homes noted in history from cave dwellings to mansions on the waterfront. Where you live is your preference, but getting a mortgage on it is up to the banks. Whatever your house is, may it be your home.

Oh, the Places People Live In!

To obtain a residential mortgage, the real property must be a co-op, condo, single-family home, or a multi-unit property no more than four units. Townhomes, log homes, and modular (pre-built) homes may also obtain financing through conventional means.

There are some special types of homes that are not typical and would need a lender that provides specialized financing. Most conventional banks will not lend on the following:

- Single or doublewide trailers
- Geo-thermal houses
- Farms
- Timeshares

- Condotels
- Round or dome houses

Occupancy of the Property Matters

Owner-occupied: This is considered your primary residence and is physically occupied by you. If a unit in a multi-family home is occupied, it is still considered a primary residence even if rental income is received from the other units. A primary residence carries the least risk in default, so it has the lowest interest rate.

Some people try to tell the bank the house will be owner-occupied when it is really an investment property in order to get a lower interest rate. Through the years, the banks have caught on and do the following litmus test:

- It must be occupied for a major portion of the year.

- It is conveniently located to place of work.

- It is the mailing address for bank accounts, tax returns, and driver's license.

- It is the intent of the borrower to occupy the home, and she signs an affidavit as such.

Second home: Most banks will only allow a second home to be a single-family house, although some lenders will allow a two-family as well. The home must be far enough away from the borrower's primary residence and located in a place that is atypical of second homes. A reasonable distance should be 30 miles or more, but again the lender will also look at the use and motivation for the property ownership. The home must be livable all year long (have proper heating and water) and not subject to any rental requirements. Most lenders will offer the same interest rate for second homes as a primary, so make sure you do not pay extra.

Investment property: A condominium, co-op, single- or multi-unit dwelling may be owned as an investment property. This home may be occupied by a paying or nonpaying tenant. If rental income is received, it will be added to salary to calculate income qualifications. An investment property is considered the riskiest of ownership due. When times get tough, a property owner is more apt to walk away from investment property than her primary residence. Therefore, the lenders will require a greater down payment and charge a higher interest rate for investor-owned properties.

Each property type has its own special nuances as well as rules for mortgage approval. However, under the new rules of mortgages, the guidelines are stricter and the interest rates reflect the risks of each property type.

Single-Family Home

You know what this is! Included in this property type are condo-miniums, co-ops, mother-daughter homes, houses with professional offices attached, and professional apartments in urban dwellings. Although the interest rate will be calculated for each as a single-family house, the mortgage processing is different. In addition, the appraisal obtained on each type will be required to include further and specific information.

Two- to Four-Unit Mortgages

A multi-unit home loan holds greater risk to the lender due to the nature of it being a rental property, whether the owner occupies a unit or simply owns it completely as an investment property. For lending purposes, a two-family is less risky than a three- or four-unit is and therefore is easier to be approved. The lender will allow a higher loan-to-value (LTV) on a two-family and will charge less for them, too. The idea is that in case of foreclosure, it will be easier for the bank to manage and sell the two-unit house.

The lender will qualify you for the loan based on your salary plus 75 percent of the rental income. If you live in one of the units, that rental income will not be used; however, the rate will be priced on an owner-occupied rate. If you are not living there, they will use all the units to calculate the rental income, but your rate and cost will be higher due to investor risk.

Townhouse

This is simply a house attached to at least one other house. It can be attached side by side or top and bottom. It may also be a row house and part of many houses or a cluster home and attached to several in a configuration. Anyway, it is considered a single-family house for lending and can be a primary, second home, or investment. Additional information will be obtained if the home is part of a planned unit development (PUD) and has special assessments or occupancy rules.

Mother-Daughter Home

An apartment within a house that uses the same entrance for access qualifies as a single-family home. It could be a small apartment in the basement or attic occupied by a family member. If the apartment is as large as the main living area, has a separate entrance, or has a paying tenant, it will not qualify. When doing the appraisal, the appraiser should have access to the apartment from the main home. Some people block it completely, and you will have to open the access again.

Professional Office

This is where a single-family home has space that is used for non-residential use. Think of a dentist, chiropractor, childcare facility, or insurance office. The owner must reside there as a primary residence and also own and manage the occupying business. The appraisal must note that the area is a legally zoned use and there is direct access from the living quarters. The value should not be significantly higher because of the use; however, this is a good selling feature if someone is looking for it.

Log Home

A log home can look like a log cabin from the outside, but the interior must be finished, insulated, and properly heated. It must also be usual and customary to the area and have several other log homes used as comparables in the appraisal. In case the borrower defaults, the bank wants to know there is a market for the house.

Modular Home

A modular home is built in sections in a factory, but then transferred to a site and put together. It will have all the proper utilities hooked up and the home will look like any regular home when put together. Any lender will do a purchase or refinance loan for a one- to four-unit modular home as long as it is put together. The problem lies when a construction loan is needed to buy and put together the modular home. A construction loan is only for real property, and the modular does not become "real" until it is together. The seller of the home wants to be paid before they take the parts off the truck curbside; therefore it takes a special lender to do a construction loan for modular home!

Co-Op

A co-op is an apartment in a building owned by a corporation. The owner of the individual unit gets a stock certificate for shares in the corporation that owns the building and a proprietary lease to occupy his unit. Thus, the person owns a percentage of the corporation, which owns the building he lives in, and has a lease with the corporation to occupy the unit. All owners collectively own the common areas and share expenses for maintenance. Maintenance includes charges for services common to all and a percentage share of the real estate taxes for the entire building. The number of shares for each unit is determined by square footage as well as how high up. A bigger apartment on a higher floor is worth more and has more shares.

Co-ops have long lists of rules about subletting, pets, and selling the units, whereas a condominium might not. People have aversions to buying in co-ops because of the rules and the approval process to buy in. However, although a hassle, a co-op is nice to buy because they are typically less expensive and the closing costs are considerably less than condos.

Apartments in Small Buildings

Many lenders will not do co-op or condo loans in buildings with less than five units. These are often found in large cities and need a specialized lender.

A co-op will want to approve potential buyers because their neighbors are shareholders in the company rather than landowners. Therefore, they want to make sure they are a good fit financially and personally. The realtor is the best source of information as to the approval process and occupant type. If it sounds like it will not be a good fit for you, then avoid even looking at the building.

Your realtor will be able to answer questions on subletting, pets, and what type of people live there. Your attorney will receive copies of the financial statements and by-laws and make sure the company is sound and financially stable. The bank will do a more extensive review of the financials as well as other items. They will look at number of owner-occupied units, insurance, mortgage on the building, and amount in reserves. If the lender rejects the building, you may want to consider living elsewhere.

Special Approval for Co-Ops Is Required

The lender will process the borrower part of the loan application as they would for any other loan; however, the co-operative building and corporation will require an extra layer of approval. For the lenders that do co-op loans, this is simply protocol; but for the borrower this can create additional stress, time, and money. To understand what has to be done, I have listed some of the most important things the bank looks for.

Prior two years of audited financial statements for the co-op corporation: They might also request a copy of the current or proposed budget to make sure there will be enough income to operate.

Underlying mortgage: A co-op corporation usually has a mortgage on the entire building, which each unit pays a share of included in their monthly maintenance. The unit's portion should not be more than 30 percent of its appraised value, nor should the mortgage be due in less than three years without provisions to pay it off or refinance it.

Proprietary lease and proposed stock certificate: The lender will want to see this for the unit before the closing in order to make sure that the lease term is not less than the mortgage term and that the name on the stock certificate will match the name on the mortgage.

Master insurance policy: There needs to be a master insurance policy for the building that covers $1 million general liability/$2 million each occurrence per incident, full replacement coverage for boilers, flood insurance (yes, NYC apartments need this, too), and wind insurance (for those tall building in urban areas). The lender will also require insurance for loss of income in case nobody pays their monthly maintenance fees, and a Fidelity Bond in case the people in the management office abscond with all the money!

Questionnaire: A questionnaire must be completed by the management company with a laundry list of things they need to know. Here are a few: How many units in the building are owner-occupied? Are 10 percent of the units owned by the sponsor or by one entity? Are any apartments overdue on their monthly maintenance payments? How big is the underlying mortgage on the building and when it is due? Is there enough insurance on the building? Are there any pending law suits?

All these things are a pain to gather, so the realtor and attorney do most of the work for you. If you are refinancing a mortgage, you should already have these items as an owner. The co-op questionnaire is now different for each bank and they demand that their own form be completed. The management office wants to use their own and charges a fee to fill out any form and provide financials. These offices are usually run by a bunch of overworked, grouchy people, so patience is a virtue.

Things you need to know about co-ops:

Flip tax: This is a charge imposed by the co-op corporation on sellers of units. It is either a percentage of the current market value, price per share, or a flat fee. This is a form of revenue for the corporation and helps fund the reserve accounts. If the flip tax is more than 3 percent of the sale price, it must be deducted from the top when calculating the mortgage; if it is less, then the actual sale price is used. A borrower needs to know the flip tax, which can be found on the first page of the sales contract, to make sure her loan amount will not be reduced.

Recognition agreement: This form is from the lender and signed by the co-op board. It gives notice to all parties that the bank has a priority lien on the unit's stock in case of default. The borrower will receive it before the closing and must have it signed in triplicate and returned prior to or at the loan closing.

UCC-1 lien search: This search is completed on the seller, borrower, and building prior to the closing. It would show any liens or judgments, or building violations that would take priority over the lender's mortgage. It also shows that the owner is who she says she is.

Board approval: A buyer as a rule needs to be approved by the co-op board. This approval process can be arduous and aggravating, but it is mandatory to make sure the owners are a good fit. A board application will need to be completed; this is similar to the mortgage application, so have the documents handy for both. In addition, personal references and some other items need to be included. Your realtor will know what to do and should help in this process.

The application package must be complete at submission, and will be returned if not. Once the application is accepted and reviewed, the board will send a notice for a face-to-face interview. If you get to the interview part, they probably approved you and just want to meet. They might also request that you bring anybody else (children, pets, etc.) living in the unit. The fact that they can request anything they want and then reject you for any reason is the big turn-off. Although it is against the law to reject someone because of race, religion, age, gender, sexual preference, or profession, they can reject you without providing a reason. Unfortunately, this is prejudice at the highest level and has been fought and lost in courts many times. If this happens, all fees you paid for the board approval and appraisal are lost, and you will have to start over. The good news is that your mortgage approval will be good for any co-op you are approved for and buy.

Condominiums

A condo is an apartment in a building or an attached townhome (PUD) that's individually owned and occupied, complete with a deed just like a house. Each unit owns a percentage of common-use areas, such as the lobby, hallways, roof, and exterior as well as the common grounds, parking lot, and garage. Therefore, in addition to your loan and real estate taxes, you will also have to pay a fee, better known as a *common charge*, to maintain the building and grounds as well as any recreational facilities. This fee is added to your housing expense when your lender is calculating your housing ratios. A lender will allow loans for primary, second home, and investment properties. The requirements are less strict than co-op loans because the condo is real property rather than shares in a corporation and thus less risky.

Special Approval for the Condo

Corporate financials: The lender needs to see the last two years of audited financials and proposed budget to make sure the company is stable. In addition, the lender requires that the homeowner's association be controlled by the owners (not the builder) and managed by an outside agency or experienced person.

Master insurance policy: Just as a co-op, the lender wants the condo corporation fully insured for liability, damage, and theft.

Condo questionnaire: The lender requires that a questionnaire be completed, covering occupancy, completion of project, common areas, all units being current on payments, pending lawsuits, and any special circumstances. Under the new rules of mortgages, lenders require the project to be 100 percent completed and not have additional sections to be queued for future construction. In case there is builder bankruptcy, the lender wants to make sure the project is not left incomplete or with cranes all over.

Board approval: A buyer usually does not need go through as intense an approval process with a condo; however, in some buildings there is some approval necessary. Perhaps a board application must be completed with personal financials. Almost never will a meeting be required.

New Rules for Condos and Co-Ops

With the collapse of the real estate market and tightening of the mortgage industry, guidelines have seriously tightened. Fearing project defaults, especially in new construction, lenders have imposed many new restrictions on project approval. A few of the major ones are these:

- The building or development must be 100 percent complete, including all common areas.

- The units must be at least 90 percent sold, closed, or under contract in a condo. For a co-op, the minimum number of sold and closed is 51 percent, although some lenders might allow fewer or require more.

- The maximum loan to value is 80 to 90 percent, depending on the project.

- No single entity owns more than 10 percent of the units.

- Units are controlled by a homeowner's association and not by a developer.

- Each lender will limit the lending exposure in a building by putting a cap on the number of units or percentage he or she will give owner mortgages to. In the case of financial ruin, the bank will not take the entire fall.

The Differences between Condos and Co-Ops

Condo	Co-Op
Real property	Corporation owns building
You own right to occupy the unit	You own shares in corporation that owns the building
Get a deed	Receive stock certificate and proprietary lease to rent the unit you live in from the building
Pay common charges such as your percentage of upkeep and maintenance of the building based on your square footage	Pay maintenance including common charges, your part of the real estate taxes, insurance, and mortgage interest paid for the whole building
Usually no board approval	Need to go before board for approval to purchase and sometimes even refinance

continues

The Differences between Condos and Co-Ops   (continued)

Condo	Co-Op
Can sublet apartment and have pets	Strict guidelines for subletting and pets
No minimum down payment	The board dictates minimum down payment, income, and post closing reserves
Can be handled by all lenders	Limited number of lenders for co-op loans

Renegade Theory

In large urban cities, there is something called the Renegade Theory. A "renegade" is defined as one of the first on the scene. With the stricter rules, it is harder to get mortgages in many projects, especially new construction. So if the building is in bad shape financially and has a large investor ownership, it might be harder to get good financing.

If it is difficult to get financing, the units should be priced lower to entice buyers who can come up with alternative financing. Alternatives are higher interest rates on private loans, lenders that specialize in these buildings, or cash. The building could be in an up-and-coming area.

Many new projects have lost buyers who ran for the hills leaving their down payments behind. In recent times, people lost assets, jobs, or could not sell their current home. In any case, there were many unsold properties back on the market, creating a large inventory of newly built homes in new areas. With so many builders being stuck, the incentive to unload properties and raise capital is sparking fire sales.

If you can get into a project and wait it out, it could pay off remarkably in the end. This is what my mother calls a "diamond in the rough." I say if you have the tolerance for risk, go for it. Do your research and it just might pay off for you!

Condop

A condop (or "cond-op") is a building that has co-op ownership with condominium rules. Compared with a co-op, getting board approval for unit ownership is easier, and the down payment is lower because a condop is easier to sell and hence less risky for the lender. Condops also have less rigid rules on subletting, pets, and other tenuous issues compared with co-ops. Closing costs will be similar to a co-op, and maintenance will be paid on a share basis for taxes, the underlying mortgage, and other building expenses. Shares are based on the number of square feet in your unit. Condops are more popular in large urban areas like Manhattan and Chicago and are probably unheard of elsewhere.

Condotels

A condotel is a condominium in a resort or hotel. Many of the high-end hotel chains have units owned by individuals. Typically, they are located in resort areas; however, during the boom they became popular in urban areas like Hoboken, New Jersey. Owners can occupy them or rent them out. The in-house management company will typically charge a fee equal to 50 percent of the rent. Residents and their renters get the use of the facilities and amenities, which can be at all levels of luxury. It is kind of the new and improved time-share because you can actually own the unit, not just rent a week or two of use, and can transfer/exchange for use in other properties.

Most banks won't give out mortgages for this type of set-up—it's too risky for them because they're essentially giving out a loan for a hotel room. Those that do give out condotel mortgages charge higher interest rates and require higher down payments than for, say, condos.

Personally, I do not see the point in these and am sure the novelty of ownership wears thin quickly.

Under the new rules for mortgages, it is nearly impossible to get financing for the condotel. Unless the building is self-financed or you are paying cash, you might want to contact a sovereign fund for a loan.

Vacant Land Loans

Vacant land loans are unique in that there is no real (property) security for the loan other than its equity. Lenders that do construction loans might also do land loans. Criteria to compare are down payment requirements, term of the loan, and balloon programs (early repayment).

Banks will give a vacant land loan with the assumption that it will be rolled into a construction loan within a few years. They don't want to hold onto a loan for land that's not going to be developed because undeveloped land is difficult to sell in a foreclosure. It is also not a real moneymaker until it is rolled into the larger construction loan or permanent loan and can be pooled and sold. Hence, the incentive of the balloon is to proceed or pay it off.

It's sometimes smarter to get a short-term loan from the seller, even if the interest rate is higher, or to take equity out of something else and buy the land for cash. It's a lot less hassle and closing costs are significantly less.

Homes with Wheels?

A few years ago, I was in Ogunquit, Maine, for Labor Day weekend. Despite the rain, the coastline was magnificent and the trip was quite relaxing (for hard-core New Yorkers).

While eating lobster rolls and watching the eagles fly, we noticed there were hordes of beautiful mobile homes on blocks right at water's edge. These homes were too big to drive up the highway, but too small to be called a "house." They were *manufactured houses*.

A manufactured house is a home that is built in a factory, transported, and then fixed to a permanent home site. It is attached to a permanent foundation and hooked up to water and utilities. It cannot be driven off into the night (although I am sure if there's a will, there's a way).

Fannie Mae and Freddie Mac will both buy loans for manufactured homes, but not all banks will do them. There are certain guidelines that must be met. The following are a few important ones:

- The size of the home must be no less than 12 feet wide and have 200 square feet of livable space.
- It cannot have its wheels on.
- It must be affixed to a permanent foundation and hooked up to septic, water, and utilities.
- It must be a primary or second home (no investor).
- It must meet local and federal building codes.

The banks that do lend for these homes will have their own layers of guidelines, so you need to check with the lender to learn about them. Also check for types of loans offered (30-years fixed, etc.), interest rates, LTVs, and add-ons for property type.

My biggest beef is that a manufactured home is classified as poor- to lower-middle-income housing, but many lenders will not do these loans, or they charge extra for them. I have issue with this because, again, the lower-income people are being overcharged, and I have seen some very expensive manufactured homes, so I don't think they are all for lower-income buyers.

As a footnote, if your home is too small, or still has its wheels on, it is classified as a mobile home. A mobile home is not considered real estate, but personal property. Think of it as a car with a bathroom! In this case, I would call a bank that might do boat loans or car loans. A broker might not be experienced in these loans and will add an extra layer of fees, so go directly to a bank.

Multi-Family Investment Loans

A mortgage on a property with five or more residential units is a "commercial" loan, regardless of whether the owner lives in one of the units. A mixed-use property with retail and residential units is commercial whether investor or owner-occupied. This loan is not the same as a residential loan in either the lending process or products offered. It is imperative to use an experienced person when getting a commercial mortgage and to comparison shop for fees and rates.

There are many differences in these mortgages from residential loans. Following are a few major things to consider:

- Debt-to-income ratio is calculated on rental income alone and the buyer's personal income is not used.
- A down payment is usually 25 percent of purchase price.
- Application fees, appraisals, attorney fees, points, and other charges are higher.
- The loans are not always for 30 years and typically have balloon payments.
- The rates are often adjustable rather than fixed.
- Points are typically paid at time of commitment rather than closing.
- There are pre-payment penalties, which can be considerable.
- The margins and caps can be negotiable.
- Lenders want the property owned in the name of a corporation.

Wrap It Up

- What kind of property you choose to live in depends on your personality type and living habits desired.

- Your property type might require a lender that specializes in that kind of loan and has good rates for it. Understand the special guidelines for loan approval and pricing before you get started.

- Make sure your loan officer is familiar with doing loans for your specific property and understands your particular needs and situation. Interview him and don't be afraid to ask questions—it is your loan.

- If you are buying a single-family home with a twist, make sure it is legal and mortgageable before you sign the contracts. Ask the realtor to get you documentation proving the township knows of the use of the property, and ask if the seller has a mortgage from a conventional bank.

- If you are buying a condo or co-op, make sure that the building is sound enough that you can get a conventional mortgage. Ask for a list of the major lenders in the building and check with them for rates.

Chapter 10

Protecting Your Homeownership: Divorce, Dispute, and Death

Protecting your homeownership involves knowing what makes someone an eligible borrower. Simply put, in order to obtain financing, the borrower must be a person of sound mind and legal age in the state of ownership. There can be no discrimination for gender, race, religion, or maximum age. A person is defined as a natural person (real and breathing) or a trust, but cannot be a corporation or partnership. Moreover, how you take legal title to your home will determine how protected your ownership is in the property. Taking title is how you own the home: alone; with another person; or in the name of a legal entity, such as a trust or LLC. Title is also known as the deed, which is recorded in the land records office showing ownership rights to the public.

How Many Mortgages Can You Have?

There used to be no limit on the number of properties or how many mortgages one could have. Under the new rules of mortgages, the number of mortgaged properties one person can have is four, including their primary residence. A first and second/home equity mortgage count as one for this guideline. Joint ownership is considered the same as sole ownership. There will be a few lenders out there that do not adhere to this number; however, the big banks that sell to Fannie Mae will, so if it might be an issue, ask. However, one could own an infinite number of properties without mortgages.

Signing the Note and the Mortgage

A *mortgage* is the actual document that you sign when borrowing money to purchase or refinance a loan for real property. It is a lien against the real property you are using as security for the loan. The mortgage is recorded in the county clerk's office where the property is located and therefore public record for the entire world to see. Whether you are Angelina Jolie or plain Jane, anyone will be able to see the payment terms of your mortgage loan and how much you paid for your home.

The *promissory note*, commonly referred to as the *note*, is a document that requires the borrower to be responsible for the debt. It is your personal guarantee to pay the money back to the lender, regardless of the value or condition of the real property used as security. So if you miss too many payments and your home is foreclosed, you owe the difference between what the house sold for and what you still owe, if anything, or the bank will come after you for it. This is known as a *deficiency judgment*.

Who Signs the Mortgage and Who Signs the Note?

Everyone who owns the property and has their name on the deed must sign the mortgage. However, only the people providing their financial information when applying and qualifying for the loan need be on the promissory note. Obviously, if there is one person on the transaction, they will be on the deed, mortgage, loan application, and note. If there is more than one person on the transaction, then not everyone needs to be on the loan application and note.

A property owner (or buyer) applies for a mortgage using credit, income, and assets to qualify for the loan. Not all persons on the transaction will always have acceptable finances to qualify for the loan. Let's say there are two buyers in a transaction—one person has great credit and makes enough income to qualify for the mortgage, and the other person has bad credit and no job. The first person may qualify for the loan on his own and therefore be enough to obtain the financing. The other person, still a buyer, is not needed to be added for him to qualify for the loan. Thus, person number one is on the deed, mortgage, loan application, and note. Person number two is on the deed and mortgage only.

I am making a big deal about this because some folks do not realize that when they buy property with another, they could be setting themselves up for trouble in case there is an ownership or relationship problem down the road.

Documents and Responsibility

The mortgage will be signed by all property owners at the closing and is sent to town hall for recording. Eventually, the document is officially stamped and a copy is sent to you or your lawyer for safekeeping. Make sure it is recorded and someone has it within six months of the closing (there are time lags in these offices). At closing, you will also sign one original promissory note and several photocopies. *Make sure that there is only one original and all the others are clearly labeled as "copies." Otherwise, you can owe a lot more than you should.*

When you pay off your loan, by either refinancing with another lender or simply paying it off in full with your lottery winnings, you should *make sure you get the original note back from the lender.* The lender is supposed to keep the document in a safe place; however, lenders lose them all the time. (I know that comes as a surprise!) If your lender does lose the originals, you can get a certified copy of the note, which is just as good as the original. The copy you receive should be accompanied by a letter that states it is a *certified* copy and the note is paid in full. Again, keep it in a safe place for your records.

Tenants in Common

A tenancy in common is where you and at least one other person decide to take title to the property together. You can either share equal title to the property or take it in different distributions. Each of you has the right to use and enjoy the entire property, not just the percentage you own. You can sell your share without the permission of the other party.

Upon your death, your portion of the property goes to your heirs. This is a common form of title for business partners and unmarried people.

But watch out, there are certain things to consider. For example, what if George and Dick buy a four-family house in Brooklyn and George dies? Dick and Laura (George's wife) now own the house together. If this is not the outcome you want, you need to make other provisions.

Joint Tenants

A joint tenancy is an arrangement in which you and at least one other person take joint title to the property.

In order to create a joint tenancy, four criteria must be met by all owners:

1. Take title at the same time.
2. Have identical title to the property.

3. Have equal ownership interest (i.e., if there are two tenants, they must share ownership 50-50).

4. Have the right to take possession of the whole property.

The unique characteristic with this form of ownership is the right of survivorship, meaning no owner may sell/transfer his or her interest. If an owner dies, the other owners(s) get the whole property immediately and automatically.

To further protect unmarried people who own property together as tenants in common or joint tenants, I suggest three additional things:

- Put your ownership percentages in the body of the deed. Frank owns 60 percent and Thomas owns 40 percent. The deed is a recorded legal document and is public record of intent.

- Create a property agreement outlining ownership; rights duties; and what will happen if one owner dies, wants to sell, or if the partnership splits up. This way your intent is outlined for all partners to reference.

- Prepare a will stating who should get your share upon death. With joint tenants, it is always the other owner(s). If you split up or transfer partial ownership to another person, update the will as well.

There are other, more detailed instructions for married couples and long-term committed relationships that are not marriages, which I will discuss later; but these special details are ones people entering into a Joint Tenancy should keep in mind.

Tenants by the Entirety

A tenancy by the entirety is a joint tenancy plus marriage. The same four criteria of a joint tenancy must be met, and the couple must be married. If two married people acquire property together, most states will presume a tenancy by the entirety was created. The same right of survivorship rule applies with this form of title. However, neither tenant may sell his or her share without the consent of the other tenant. These are the terms, in a nutshell:

- You must acquire interest in the property at the same time.
- You will share equal ownership.
- You will have equal rights of possession.
- You must be a legally married man and woman.

The benefit of this form of title is that a judgment creditor cannot place a lien on the home for the debts of one spouse. If the deadbeat dies first, the property goes automatically to the clean one. If the clean one goes first, the creditors can go after the house.

Upon divorce, property ownership automatically reverts to tenants in common, and you can do whatever you want with your share.

The Trust Agreement

Not all lenders will give you a loan in the name of a trust. It is difficult to foreclose or sue a trust, and lenders will be very cautious. There are some that will do it; however, they will charge a premium buried in a higher interest rate or points, and they will want the trustee to also sign personally for the mortgage.

The living trust or intervivos trust is allowed, so find out what the terms are from your attorney. From experience, this is not an easy loan to get, so do your research first on lenders, fees, rate premiums, and documentation required.

A living trust is one that can be revocable by the creator of the trust. This trust used to be for the rich to protect their assets from probate taxes upon death. Now, many people use this as a vehicle to pass assets to their heirs and avoid probate. For mortgage purposes, the trust must be revocable, so check for those terms before applying for the loan.

Corporations, Partnerships, and LLCs

Although these are perfectly acceptable ways to own property, obtaining financing for residential properties will pose a problem. Most lenders will not lend to these entities due to difficulty in foreclosing. Again, some local lenders will permit corporate ownership but the big boys that sell to Fannie Mae will not.

Corporation: This legal entity has individual owners in the form of stockholders. The owners have no personal liability and share in profits in the form of dividends and stock value. The corporation is legally responsible and liable for all actions of the company.

Partnership: This is a legal entity where the partners share ownership and profits as natural persons. Unlike a corporation, the profits and losses pass through to the partners for tax purposes to be dealt with on their personal returns.

Limited liability company (LLC): This company has members instead of shareholders. It is a hybrid of both corporation and partnership rules. The LLC protects the members from liability of corporate actions while passing income through as a partnership would. It is the cool thing to have, but it's not as strong a shield as one might think, because if someone wants to sue you, he can.

If you are only worried about personal liability, insurance is the way to go, instead of going to the trouble of an LLC. Get good homeowners' insurance, even if you have to get a high deductible. If you have investment property, get an umbrella policy. This policy is a separate policy that ensures all owned assets—such as houses and cars—are insured in case of major catastrophe. You will sleep much better under the shade of your umbrella because it will protect your primary residence and other assets from lawsuits.

If a person owned property as an individual and then transferred ownership to an entity, he will be able to refinance the mortgage, but only after the title is transferred back to the individual. The lender will require proof that he owned the property before the transfer and he was making payments on the mortgage through the entity. Of course, he would still be personally obligated to pay the new mortgage payments and personally liable for any problems with the home.

Due on Sale Clause

There have been known transactions where people buy properties in their personal names, close on a mortgage, and then transfer it to a corporation. They think they are being sly, but it is illegal.

Technically, you cannot do that and will have to repay the loan to the lender. There is a "due on sale" clause written into every mortgage loan agreement that says if you transfer ownership, the loan is due and payable. By transferring it to your LLC, you have triggered the due on sale clause and must pay back the loan.

Historically, however, lenders were not so quick to ask for their money back or foreclose if you had been paying the loan back on a timely basis. Furthermore, your loan had probably already been sold several times and is part of a servicing pool. It probably got lost in the pool, but as long as you were paying on time, nobody cared. *Just know that I am not telling you to do this, or that you will get away with it today.*

Unconventional Housing Situations

There will always be home ownership situations which require an extra layer of protection and need to be well thought out in the beginning. I have given you three unusual examples next. Although my stories are extreme and humorous, there is nothing funny about protecting your rights as a property owner. Proper guidance and documentation can save much aggravation and money in the long run, so please make sure you cover yourself when everybody is still happy and in love.

Meet My Significant Other

Bill and Bob are happily together for 20 years and decide to buy a vacation home together in Woodstock, New York. Bill's credit is perfect: he has a great income and a fat 401(k). Meanwhile, Bob's finances are not as pretty as his smile, so he doesn't qualify for a mortgage. Bill takes title and applies for the mortgage alone. They go on the assumption that it's their house, and they enjoy it together for five years, sharing the expenses and joys of homeownership. One stormy night on his way up from Manhattan, Bill dies in a car accident.

Not caring about his relationship with Bob, his parents come to the house to clean it out and put it up for sale. After 25 long years of bliss and happiness, Bob is homeless.

If Bill and Bob had thought about it beforehand, they could have saved each other heartache by owning the house as joint tenants with the right of survivorship. They should also have prepared a real property agreement stating the terms of ownership and what should occur in the case of death, breaking up, or forced sale of property. Lastly, each should have prepared wills including the real estate. The court will protect the partners if their wishes are laid out clearly in the legal documents.

In states where same-sex marriage is legal, it is still a safe assumption that the right could be repealed at a later date. For this reason, I would strongly recommend a legally married same-sex couple not assume they automatically take ownership as tenants by the entirety. I would advise taking title as joint tenants with right of survivorship and taking every precaution listed previously.

The Model and the Fool

Here is some advice for the fool in love. As we learned previously, if two people are on the contract, they are both on the deed and sign the mortgage as well. However, if one of them is much more credit-worthy than the other, that person can be on the loan application alone and will also sign the note alone.

Here, our model is beautiful and dumb like a fox, and our fool is well educated yet naïve. The happy couple goes to the closing and the model signs the mortgage and few other documents. The fool signs the mortgage, promissory note (alone), and all the other documents. *Signing the note alone makes the fool solely responsible for making the payments.*

A few months after they move into the home, things get a little shaky and the model begins an affair. After finding out, the fool is so heart-broken that he moves out of the house. They agree that the model will remain in the home and make the mortgage payments from her own income. For the next six months, the model neglects to make the payments on the loan. The bank begins foreclosure proceedings and sends notice to the house. The fool does not know about this because the fool no longer lives there. The bank ends up foreclosing and takes the house. Whom does the bank go after on the personal note? The fool, because the fool is financially responsible.

The Old Man and Much Younger Woman

Most attorneys and homebuyers assume married couples automati-cally take ownership as tenants by entirety. They do not have to, and it is not always the best strategy.

An old man marries his masseuse; he is 80, and she is 25. He buys a huge house on the Gold Coast of Miami and she insists on being on the deed. His children throw a fit because Dad used most of his cash (their inheritance) to buy the home, and this will now be the major asset in his estate. If she is on the deed and he dies first, she will get the entire property. The wife insists, and after much negotiation, the father relents and agrees to let her on the deed as a 10 percent owner. They take title as tenants in common. If he dies first, his share goes to his heirs, and she owns 10 percent. Still a bad situation, but they will be able to buy her out.

The Amicable Divorce

The laziest mistake a divorce attorney can make is letting one spouse keep the house and take the other off the deed, but allowing the mortgage to remain in both names just because the parties are on good terms with each other. If you are on the mortgage, you're responsible for the payments whether you live there or not, and whether the house is physically yours or not. So if you are the one thrown out, make sure your ex refinances and gets a mortgage in his or her own name without yours before you take your name off the deed. It does not matter that it's in the divorce agreement that you're not responsible for the loan payments. The lender doesn't care what the two of you have personally agreed to. In the case of foreclosure, both of you will be liable.

While we're on the topic, if you're divorcing, you should close all joint credit accounts. Otherwise, the full debt will be included in both spouses' liabilities. I recommend cutting all financial ties with an ex, because you never know when it's going to come back to bite you.

Usually, exes move on and buy new homes or take on new obligations before the divorce papers are filed. Lenders will continue to add all the debt into your liability until your joint accounts are completely closed and removed. Try to pay off and close as many joint accounts as possible. When buying the marital home from the other, the bank will require a Separation Agreement outlining the detailed financial arrangement.

Special Purpose Refinances

I really get into this topic in Chapter 11, but it merits mention here. A person may refinance an existing mortgage up to 90 percent of the value if he needs the proceeds to pay off an ex or a co-owner. He must provide proof of ownership and the deal made between parties. The one being paid off must sign over her ownership at or before the closing and provide proof that she received the money. A copy of the separation or property agreement, deed, revised deed, and closing statement will do the trick. Under the new rules for mortgages, lenders are looking for more final deals, such as signed and recorded separation agreements. They might also request supporting documentation saying that the terms are final and not subject to change. This request does not make attorneys too happy.

Transferring the Title

A homeowner wants to transfer the title to the house to his son. He is going to assume the mortgage and start making the payments to the lender. He is also going to get his own insurance and pay the taxes directly to the tax receiver's office. The homeowner wants to do this for estate purposes, so if something should happen to him, the house is already in his son's name.

I need to preface this by saying: you *cannot* do this! Again, you cannot simply decide to transfer ownership, even if it's to a family member. This is the same as selling the property, so your son will have to get a loan in his own name the day the ownership is transferred. Again, if you do this without notifying the bank, and if he makes every payment on time and you do not die, who's to know? One missed payment and it shows up on your credit report, so it might not be worth the easy way out.

Adding a Person to the Deed

You're getting divorced and taking your husband off the deed and putting your new boyfriend on. If you're remaining on the title, taking the ex off, and putting the new guy on, this is a refinance. At least one person (you) remains on the title to show continuity of obligation to pay the mortgage. The loan application is completed in your name and your boyfriend's name. On the day of the closing, a new deed is filed from you and your ex to you and your boyfriend, you both (you and the new guy) sign the note and mortgage, and your ex is effectively off the title. Obviously, the ex needs to know and probably wants something for signing it over. This is where the divorce lawyer gets involved.

Please note that if you marry your boyfriend, you will not own the property as tenants by the entirety, so make provisions for joint ownership prior to the first transaction. This also works for adding a family member or friend on the deed. As long as one original owner remains on the deed, it is always a refinance to the bank.

Wrap It Up

- Make sure you understand and discuss how you are taking title and that all parties will be equally protected.
- It is smart to have all property owners also be equally responsible for the promissory note, but if that is impossible, then make sure all parties are protected.
- If you need to buy property in the name of a trust or corporation, shop for a lender far in advance, have all of your legal documents available to show the lender before you begin the mortgage process, and understand the terms of the mortgage.
- If a relationship is ending, make sure that property ownership and all joint liability is severed legally and responsibly.
- It is illegal to transfer the title to property or add someone to it without notifying the bank and adding her onto the mortgage.
- Change your will to reflect the current property and ownership status.

Chapter 11

You Are a Homeowner!

Congratulations! You own your very own home; now what do you do? A house is probably the largest asset most people will have in their portfolio, and it is important to maintain it in tip-top shape. As part of your net worth, you want to make sure that your asset is not a liability.

Healthy Equity

There are two schools of thought here. One is to leverage your home as high as you can to keep your assets liquid as well as take advantage of tax write-offs. The other school is to pay off your mortgage as quickly as possible so you can get debt free and have your overhead as low as possible for those golden years. Either choice is fine, as long as it is done for the right reasons and correctly performed.

Things to consider would be your age and how close you are to retirement, whether you have multiple children you need to put through college, whether you own a second home, what your other large debts are, and how big your liquid portfolio is. I personally come from the second school here. There is nothing more comforting than knowing the place you call home will never be felt as a burden.

Maintain Proper Insurance

Homeowner's insurance is required to protect the homeowner as well as the lender, and is therefore a necessary expense. Theft, liability, fire, and flood are all disasters that can bankrupt and devastate, so pay the premiums. In order to close on a mortgage, the lender requires that a policy be in effect and paid for at least six months. Each year, the lender will get a copy of a paid receipt showing that insurance is still in effect.

Because insurance premiums increase each year, I suggest comparison shopping around the time of renewal. There are many new companies and plans created each year. For instance, a company might be new to your state and will enter with very low premiums just to get a market share. Check around and even use an insurance agent to do the shopping for you. You might need to increase your deductible (e.g., to reduce your premium). So your premium would be lower, but if there is an incident, you pay more out of pocket. Some states have a minimum deductible allowed; you should check with your agent about this. I myself use an insurance broker and shop health, homeowner, and car insurance each year.

Look Down the Road

In the past five years, the burden of real estate taxes and insurance has gone up significantly. You need to look into the future to see if the home you want to buy will still be affordable down the road with estimated increases in taxes, insurance, and utilities. You can do research by going to the town records to see what the increases have been over the past 10 years and ask if the town is considering an increase in the near future.

A good rule of thumb is to assume a 5 percent housing expense increase each year. Lenders currently do not take into consideration potential increases, but they might in the near future.

Hidden Money Savers

States and counties have various money savers out there, such as tax abatements, discounts, and special assessments, but you'll have to dig around to find them. It could be a small windfall in savings. Call the tax assessor's office or go down there to speak to someone.

In New York, for example, the Star Exemption program allows homeowners to deduct the first $30,000 to $60,000 in value from the school tax assessment. Florida has a Full Value Homestead Tax Exemption. (This is different from the homestead exemption that protects your home if you are sued.) All states and counties have some sort of discounts for the blind, widowed, disabled, ex-service member, permanently disabled, and senior citizens. Seek and you shall find!

Keep That House Pretty

Statistics show the first thing people look at when house shopping are the kitchen and bathrooms. When putting money into cosmetic upgrades, remember, you will not get that equal return on your investment. In other words, if you spend $50,000 on a new kitchen with granite countertops and high-end cherry wood cabinets, you will not increase the value (or price) of the home by $50,000. In fact, you might not get any increase at all, so think before you spend— especially if you are not planning to stay long.

Again, statistics show curb appeal has huge value. A house with a clean yard and nice landscaping might get a 10 percent boost in sale price. Why a tree and not a cherry wood cabinet? Perhaps because the yard is really the first thing people see when they pull up to the curb and a cherry or oak door does not really matter. Clean up that yard!

Moving on Up

Eventually people want to move, whether it's because they need to, outgrew their home, or plain got tired of it. In any case, most people have to sell their home in order to buy a new one, so get your ducks in order before you move forward.

- Where do you want to move?
- What is the price range of the new house?
- What is your timeframe or deadline to move?
- Is your financial profile still in order?
- Have you interviewed listing brokers for your current home to discover market values and timeframe to sell?
- How much money do you need for this purchase and how much equity will you net from the sale?

After all that, do you still want to do this?

What If You Die?

Buying a house is the best reason to write a will or update the one you have. Anybody who owns property but does not have a will is making a mistake. Even if you are legally married and own your home as tenants by the entirety, a simple will should be prepared ... in case you both go together. For those who own property otherwise, a will is mandatory to make sure everybody is covered when the time comes.

Getting a mortgage is also a good time to list all of your asset accounts, review your portfolios, consolidate accounts, or make adjustments for tax purposes. Clean up your finances just as you would the yard!

Why Refinance?

Refinancing means that you're paying off the existing mortgage with a new loan. Whatever your reason, refinancing should accomplish more than one goal. Because it is expensive and can be arduous, make sure it is worth your effort.

I believe there is no rule of thumb to the percentage of lowering your interest rate; it is about the monthly payment reduction. You might be reducing your interest rate by 1 percent, but only saving $50 a month. I also encourage a borrower to find a secondary benefit for refinancing.

Here is a list of reasons; choose at least two:

- Lower your interest rate
- Shorten your term or make it longer to reduce the monthly payment over time
- Lower/increase your monthly payments
- Consolidate mortgages and debt
- Change your rate from adjustable to fixed (or vice versa)
- Pay off part of the principle
- Take equity out of your home

Remember, refinancing should not be approached lightly, and no one of these reasons by itself is enough of a reason to refinance. What you need to do is figure out how much you are saving, what the refinancing closing costs will be, and how long it will take to recoup the expenses. For example, if you have already paid down 7 years on a mortgage, is it worth you refinancing back into a 30-year loan and paying $4,000 in closing costs just to save $100 dollars a month. I would think that if you did the math, that loan would cost you more money in the long run. In addition, if you are already down seven years, do you really want to start from the beginning again? Sometimes, it's just not worth it.

No Refi Allowed!

A refinance is not permitted on a vacant home or a multi-unit dwelling that does not have at least one unit occupied. Under the new rules for mortgages, lenders now do a litmus test to make sure there is a valid reason for refinancing, such as lowering the payment, term, or interest rate. If there is no benefit to the borrower, the loan will be rejected. Under the new rules, lenders have rejected refinancing mortgages for the following reasons:

- Avoid foreclosure
- Skim equity out of the home
- Defer making loan payments
- Churn fees for third parties
- Simply because there is no valid reason

Do not think you can outsmart the bank into giving you free money; the bank is out to protect its own interests—oh, and yours.

The Rate and Term Refinance

This loan is simply for paying off the existing mortgages and covering the closing costs. The cash out is limited to whichever is lower: 2 percent of the mortgage amount or $2,000.

A second mortgage must have been used to originally purchase the house or it will be considered cash out. Even if the terms of the second mortgage have been changed, it is still considered cash out. For example, my client took out a first and second mortgage to buy a house in Brooklyn. He had modified the second mortgage from a line of credit to a fixed rate for the same loan amount with the same lender. The new lender said this was deemed a new loan, did not meet the cash-out guidelines, and rejected his refinance.

Second Mortgages = Credit Cards

When taking a second mortgage or home equity loan for purchasing a home, make sure to use the entire amount as purchase money at the closing, even if you do not need it. Otherwise, when refinancing the second mortgage it will be considered a cash-out refinance and cost a premium.

The New Cash-Out Refinance

A cash-out refinance is a loan where, among other things, the borrower walks away with a chunk of change. We have heard many tales of people taking every last nickel of equity out of their homes. Apparently, lenders decided this was not a good thing and put restrictions on the maximum allowed for cash out and for the loan-to-value (LTV) of the new loan. The borrower must own the property for a minimum of six months. If the property is owned less than 12 months, then the LTV is based on the original purchase price. If there is no existing mortgage on the property, the transaction is still considered a cash-out refinance and the total amount of cash allowed will be capped according to individual lender guidelines. Under the new rules for mortgages, the lenders will also charge a premium for taking cash out. The amount of premium depends on the LTV and the FICO score.

For Sale: No Refi Allowed

Most banks will not allow a refi or cash-out refi on any home that has been listed for sale within the last 12 months. The premise is that the house could not sell and the owners are now pulling the equity out of the home, but if a buyer came along they would sell it. Originating mortgages is expensive and the banks are not looking for short-term investments.

The time starts from the date of the listing or the date the listing was removed, depending on the bank. They will want proof that the listing is distinguished and an explanation as to why the borrowers changed their mind and intention of staying.

Remember, if the listing was removed, it will remain in the listings that banks and appraisers use to research home values. The appraiser is obligated to state that the house was listed for sale in the last five years, so there is no way of hiding it. They think of everything you can do!

Premiums for Cash-Out Refinance*

Credit Score	<=60.00	60.01–70	70.01–75	75.01–80	80.01–85	85.01–90	90.01–95	95.01–97	97.01–100
>=740	0.000	0.250	0.250	0.500	0.625	0.625	NA	NA	NA
720–739	0.000	0.625	0.625	0.750	1.500	1.000	NA	NA	NA
700–719	0.000	0.625	0.625	0.750	1.500	1.000	NA	NA	NA
680–699	0.000	0.750	0.750	1.375	2.500	2.000	NA	NA	NA
660–679	0.250	0.750	0.750	1.500	NA	NA	NA	NA	NA
640–659	0.250	1.250	1.250	2.250	NA	NA	NA	NA	NA
620–639	0.250	1.250	1.250	2.750	NA	NA	NA	NA	NA
<620	NA	NA	NA	NA	NA	NA	NA	NA	NA

LTV Ratios

NA = Not allowed for Fannie Mae loans.

*These figures are subject to change. Use this as a guide but check with your lender for current adjustments.

When Refinancing, Lower the Term of Your Mortgage

When refinancing, always shave off a few years if you can. If you go back where you started from, you will wind up paying more interest over the life of the loan. Unless you need to make the payments lower, try to keep the payment the same, while lowering the interest rate and the term. The loan officer can do a loan comparison chart for you.

Let's look at an example: Peter took out a 30-year fixed mortgage, has been paying it off for the last 3 years and has 27 years left. He can refinance and lower his interest rate 1 percent and pay off some credit cards. Instead of taking out a new 30-year fixed loan, he opted for a 25-year loan. If he had taken out a 30-year loan, between the closing costs and the extra 3 years of interest, the refi would have cost him thousands more over the long run. Always try to reduce the term of the loan when refinancing. It will save you time and money, and make you feel good!

Lower Your Interest Rate by Accelerating Your Mortgage Payments

If the only reason you have to refinance is to lower your interest rate, you can do this yourself without going through the new loan hassle. Simply pay one extra payment a year over the life of the loan. By doing so, you'll save a third of the total interest, lowering the effective interest rate by 2 percent. You can pay off a 30-year loan in approximately 24 years, cutting off 6 years. The extra payments will also help build equity much faster.

Here's an example:

Mortgage: $300,000

6%/30-year fixed

Normal payment schedule: 360 payments for $1,798

Interest paid over the life of loan: $347,515.44

One extra payment a year made by adding $149.83 ($\frac{1}{12}$ of one payment) to each payment monthly:

Loan will be paid off in 295 months (about 24.5 years)

Interest paid over the life of loan: $273,870.87

Total savings: $73,644.57

Wrap It Up

- Are you making sure your taxes and insurance are the lowest they can be by taking advantage of any tax rebates or exemptions your municipalities offer?

- While thinking of upgrades, do your research as to cost versus the increased home value they will bring.

- When planning on moving, be sure it makes sense by doing research on selling your existing home and buying before you even begin.

- When refinancing, make sure you have a valid reason to satisfy the lender and more than one benefit to yourself for doing so.

- Do you have a will or have you updated your existing one to include the current property?

Index

C

G

H

N

O

206   The New Rules for Mortgages

Q–R

questionnaires
  condominiums, 160
  co-ops, 157

radon inspection, 76
range of FICO scores, 5
rapid rescore response, 21-23
rate and term refinance, 188
rate quotes, 134
real estate, 151
  commercial loans, 166
  condominiums, 159
    appraisals, 71-72
    building information, 129-130
    special approval requirements, 160-162
  condops, 163
  condotels, 163-164
  co-ops, 155
    appraisals and, 71-72
    building information, 129-130
    special approval requirement, 156-162
  inspection, 74-76
  limits, 170
  log homes, 155
  manufactured houses, 164-166
  modular homes, 155
  mother-daughter homes, 154
  multi-unit homes, 153-154
  occupancy
    investment properties, 152-153
    joint tenancy, 172-173
    owner-occupied, 152
    second homes, 152
  professional offices, 154

Renegade Theory, 162-163
single-family homes, 153
specialized financing properties, 151-152
townhomes, 154
vacant land loans, 164
recasting, 85
recognition agreements, co-ops, 158
refinances, 186
  appraisals and, 74
  cash-out refinance, 189
  closings, 148
  lowering interest rate, 191-192
  lowering mortgage term, 191
  rate and term refinance, 188
  rejections, 187-189
  special purpose, 179-180
rehabilitation loans, 103
removal of PMI, 81-82
Renegade Theory, 162-163
rental income, 38-41
rentals, 61-62
repayment ability (loans), 32-33
reports, credit
  agencies, 2
  alternative credit profiles, 24-25
  errors, 10
  free reports, 26-27
  immigrants, 26
  inquiries, 12-14
  other countries, 26
  review in loan process, 123-124
  tri-merge credit reports, 28
reserves, cash, 53-54
responsibilities of homeownership, 171-172
retirement income, 45